A Reference Guide for the Novice Wiccan: The Ultimate Crash Course in all things Wiccan - Wicca 101

By: Kristina Benson

A Reference Guide for the Novice Wiccan: The Ultimate Crash Course in all things Wiccan - Wicca 101

ISBN 13: 978-1-603320-16-0

TABLE OF CONTENTS

INTRODUCTION

This book is geared for the beginning Wiccan who is curious about the Craft and isn't sure where to start learning or how to become a part of the community. I have included the basics of Wicca itself, the Sabbats, crystal properties, herbalism, some basic spells, and a couple advanced practices to whet the palate for further study.

So go forth on this new path, and as you do so, remember the Wiccan Rede:

> An it harm none, do as thou wilt
> Do what you will, so long as it harms none
> An it harm none, do what thou will
> That it harm none, do as thou wilt
> Eight words the Wiccan Rede fulfill,
> An it harm none do what ye will.

WICCA 101

WHAT IS WICCA?

Wicca is a beautiful, peaceful religion that seeks to find harmony and divinity in all that surrounds us. Wicca honors the magic and majesty of the ocean, the mountains, even the sky and the air. Wicca finds divinity in the crystalline sheen of a snowflake, the smell of a meadow after the rain, the sound of the ocean crashing on the sand. Witchcraft—a word often used interchangeably with Wicca-- is a spiritual system that encourages learning and an understanding the Earth and Nature.

Wicca, in short, reveres the Earth and all she has given us. Wicca is humility in the face of nature, and seeking to tune in with the Lord and the Lady that are embodied every rock, tree, blade of grass, and animal. To practice Wicca is to a connection with the earth and all of her creatures. Wiccans believe that the spirit of the Goddess and God exist in all things. This means that we must treat the bounty of the Earth as aspects of the divine. We attempt to honor and respect life in all its many manifestations. We believe that a field of flowers is the eyes of the world.

We are not a cult, and we do not claim that ours is the True Path. We do not attempt to indoctrinate others, or persuade them to join our flocks. We do not cut them off from their friends or loved ones, and we do not tell others that their religions are wrong. Contrary to an all too popular misconception, we do not worship Satan. Satan is a creation of the Abrahamic religions of which we are not a part. Wicca and Satanism are not at all similar religions but were linked by the Christian church during the Salem Witch Trials in the colonies, and the Middle Ages in Europe.

We do the right thing not because we are scared of the eternal hellfire and damnation that await us should we do wrong. We do what is right because we believe it is, and don't need the daylights scared out of us to do so. We care deeply for animals, and we do not seek to hex or enchant or harm others. The potions we concoct and the spells we cast may be a headache remedy, a cold tonic, or a flea bath for our animal companions. We prize the natural remedies made by Mother Nature and tend to prefer them to synthetic drugs made by corporations.

Some claim that Wicca, or at least Wiccan ideologies, are derivative of the practices of Paleolithic peoples, who worshipped nature, and the God and the Goddess as guardians of the hunt and fertility, respectfully. There are also similarities between Native American Shamanism and Wicca in that both revere nature, and honor nature and the spirits of the God and Goddess. Traditional Wicca, as it tends to be practiced today, is a fairly recent phenomenon founded by Gerald Gardner, a British civil servant. He wrote a book on Celtic deities, symbols, seasonal days of celebration, and ceremonial practices. The Celtic deities, as resurrected by Gerald Gardner, form the basis of Wicca.

Practitioners of these Celtic religions had found they needed to keep their craft a great secret as Christianity swept through Europe, and the church sought to wipe out non-believers. It was at this time that aspects of Pagan culture were either demonized or absorbed into Christian tradition. Witches, for example, were made into ugly old women. Pan, the faun known for merrymaking and music, morphed into the devil. The festivities surrounding Winter Solstice (decorating an evergreen tree and spending twelve days in celebration of the winter) were eventually used celebrate the birth of Christ. Sadly, persecution and fear of Wiccans and Pagans persist to this day. Concerned parent Laura Mallory, for example, took her child's school to court for including Harry Potter in the school library, claiming that the books sought to indoctrinate children into witchcraft. In fact, according to the American Library Association, the Harry Potter books are, so far, the most challenged books of the 21st century.

Rest assured, gentle reader, that Wicca seeks to harm none. There are worse things than learning to care for and cherish Mother Nature, and honoring the Goddess and the God. This brings us to another important aspect of Wicca— who are the Goddess and the God?

Many Wiccans believe in a deity that is not definable, but still present in all living things. They feel that although the deity cannot be observed or measured, there is a definite male and femaleness, which is expressed as The Goddess, or the God and comprehend the male and female aspects of the deity, whom they call the God and the Goddess. Others relate to and worship the God or Goddess through other deities that embody whatever quality they seek to honor. For example, they might relate to Athena, Brigit, Ceridwen, Diana, Hecate, Ishtar, Isis, Venus, Selene, Apollo, Dionysus, Odin, Osiris, Pan, or Thor as embodiments of the feminine or masculine aspects of the All or the One.

Others feel that everything in nature are true aspects of the Deity and it is not necessary to personify him or her as Athena, or, say, Demeter. These are perfectly legitimate viewpoints for a Wiccan to take, however, the deities most often celebrated are the Triple Goddess of the Moon (who is Maiden, Mother, and Crone) and the Horned God of the wilds.

Though some practice alone or with only their families, many Wiccans practice in groups called Covens. Some Covens have strict rules as to who may join, and under what circumstances. Some operate as a collective authority where no one is really in charge, others rotate into leadership positions, and still others have strict, observed hierarchies. Some Covens will allow any and all interested parties to observe; others will only permit observation, much less participation, after extensive studying.

The meetings themselves may be informal gatherings in which coven members discuss challenges they are facing in their daily lives, ask for guidance, or simply talk. Others are more structured, particularly those that are in honor of a holiday of a ritual. (Holidays and rituals will be discussed later).

WHAT WICCA ISNT

Wicca is not the brand of witchcraft portrayed in Bewitched, Harry Potter, or a variety of other movies and television shows. Wiccans cannot wiggle their noses to summon the appearance of an elephant, or shout a spell in order to disarm someone of a weapon. Wiccans are not green, with hooked noses and warts, and they do not say things like "I'll get you my pretty, and your little dog too!"

Wicca is also not "Satan worship" or "devil worship". Satan is part of the Abrahamic tradition. Wiccans, by definition, are not Christian or Muslim or Jewish. Wiccans do not even believe in Satan, much less worship him.

There are many, many misconceptions about this beautiful and peaceful way of life. Most are total fabrications.

WHO CAN BE A WITCH?

Anyone, man or woman, may study the Craft and may,
after enough exposure, decide this to be the right path for
them. Women, however, hold the central place in Wicca. A
Traditional Coven is headed by a High Priestess, which is a
Third Degree female Witch with at least three years and
three days of training in addition to study. A Priest is
optional, but the Priestess is mandatory.

People often ask "Can I become a Wiccan and still remain a
Christian, Muslim, practicing Jew, etc". The answer is no,
as the Abrahamic religions in particular necessitate and
demand a belief in one god. This means that in order to be
a Christian, Muslim, or Jew, one must reject other paths
besides their own, including each other's.

To be a real witch, you must have empathy and compassion
for all peoples, animals, and spirits. In Wicca,
Unconditional Love is the most Sacred Law. It is the giving
of your heart and the core of your being to the God or
Goddess of your choice that makes you a true Witch. Even
the simplest and easiest of Spells and Rituals will not work
if your heart and purpose/intentions are not pure. Be Light
In Your Heart, And A True Witch You Shall Be.

Magick is real, it is very powerful and in the wrong hands, can be destructive. Becoming a witch is a serious decision and may eventually come to change and represent who you are. Magick is the power within you and can potentially do many things both good and bad. It takes a long time to learn and master, for Magick is a piece of every part of you. If you really want to be a Witch, be absolutely sure about it.

You also must be willing to learn and study. Spells often require the use of Sacred symbols, and Herbs, and the more you know, the more confident and magickal you are. There is no shortcut to becoming a true Witch, it takes respect for yourself, humanity for others, devotion, and lots of time and learning.

Witches are all ages, races, and nationalities. Though there is no required uniform, costume, or manner of dress, most female Wiccans prefer to wear long, flowing skirts and dresses, adorn themselves with jewelry, and keep their hair long and natural. As the Goddess is conceived of as more womanly in shape and proportion than the typical Western ideal, many Wiccan women seek to develop their shapely curves instead of exercising themselves into skin and bone. Many male Wiccans also choose to wear jewelry, keep their hair long, and select earth-toned clothing.

And, as Wiccans revere Mother Nature and the Earth, many Wiccans are active in environmental and animal-rights causes.

Though many Wiccans prefer to practice in secret, Wicca is not a members-only, exclusive community. There are plenty of web-based communities if there are no practicing Wiccans near where you live. So if you'd like to get involved, you are most likely welcome!

HOW DO I GET STARTED IN WICCA?

Wiccans believe that once can only become a true Wiccan after much preparation and study. There are a variety of resources available about Wicca, Herbalism, and natural medicine, both in print, and on the web. For example, Erica Jong has an amazing book called Witches, which explains the way that the Pagan Fertility Goddess became transformed into today's version of a witch—an ugly old lady with a pointy hat. Typing "wicca" into Amazon should lead you to a variety of sources.

Study, of course, is not just about reading books. You should also spend time alone, ideally in meditation, trying to understand what has led you to this path. Why do you want to do this? Depending on the area you live in, and how private you are about the Craft, you may experience prejudice and judgment. Are you prepared to deal with the consequences of ignorance without using anger or force? Keep a careful, meticulous notebook of your experiences as you prepare. Make note of how you feel, and how your perceptions of the world have changed since you began studying. Observe any changes that take place in your body as you become more aware of the earth and its cycles. Taking notes on what you have read will also become very useful to you later.

Hiking, swimming in the ocean, or camping may also help you get in touch with nature. Planting a garden of herbs—even if you only have space for a few plants on a windowsill—is also a must. You will find pennyroyal, lavender, and garlic of particular use, although you may, of course, select any herbs that catch your eye when researching plant properties.

It is also necessary to choose a tradition. Do a significant amount of research on all the different Goddesses and Gods before you start any works of Magick. Most Wiccan Traditions have particular roots in the British Mystery Traditions. This includes traditions of the Picts who lived before the rise of Celtic consciousness, the early Celts, and Celtic Druidism. American Wicca is directly descended from British Wicca, brought in the late 1950's by English and American Initiates of Gardnerian, Alexandrian and Celtic Wicca.

Eventually, you will want to start focusing more on the quality and length of your meditation. Taking Yoga or Tai Chi may help you. At the very least, try to meditate ten minutes a day, four days per week. Ideally, meditation should involve thinking of absolutely nothing. In practice, getting to this sort of elevated state can take decades of dedication and work, so you will probably find that your mind wanders. Write down what you think of, and why, as you meditate.

In some cultures, the use of drugs to achieve a meditative state is encouraged. Native Americans, for example, used psychoactive drugs as a religious practice and as an event marking the change from one state of life to another. Although Wicca doesn't specifically encourage the use of such drugs, it doesn't specifically forbid them either.

In addition to meditation, it's important that you work on your visualization skills. If you can visualize a personal, positive reality, you can more easily change or bring that reality into being.

Now that you've become mentally and spiritually prepared to begin the journey, you can now begin some basic work with spells and potions. These will be discussed in more detail later.

After you have been studying for at least five or six months you may perform a self dedication ritual. Design it however you want—the significance of it is very personal, because it means that you are truly ready to dedicate yourself to Wicca.

As you study, write down all that you learn. This will become your Book of Shadows. The Book of Shadows is traditionally a hand copied book of rituals, recipes, training techniques, guidelines, and other materials deemed important to a Witch or a coven. Each tradition has its own standard version of the Book and each Witch's book will be different. Only another Witch can see your book of shadows. It may never leave possession until death, when it should be destroyed by a person of your choosing, returned to the coven to be disposed of.

After the dedication, continue studying until you feel ready for initiation. Before initiation you should be familiar with the traditions and practices involved in celebrating the Sabbats, different forms of divination, such as Tarot or Runes, and different forms of healing, such as herbalism.

When indeed you are ready for initiation, if working on your own and without a coven, create your own ritual. A coven initiation is a means of bonding a group together and solidifies your dedication to the coven. Initiation into the craft, however, is very personal, and can be a solitary ritual.

THE WITCHES CREED
by Doreen Valiente

Hear now the words of the witches,
The secrets we hid in the night,
When dark was our destiny's pathway,
That now we bring forth into light.

Mysterious water and fire,
The earth and the wide-ranging air.
By hidden quintessence we know them,
And will and keep silent and dare.

The birth and rebirth of all nature,
The passing of winter and spring,
We share with the life universal,
Rejoice in the magickal ring.

Four times in the year the Great Sabbat Returns,
And the witches are seen,
At Lammas and Candlemas dancing,
On May Eve and old Hallowe'en.

When day-time and night-time are equal,
When sun is at greatest and least,
The four Lesser Sabbats are summoned,
Again witches gather in feast.

Thirteen silver moons in a year are,
Thirteen is the coven's array,
Thirteen times at esbat make merry,
For each golden year and a day.

The power was passed down the ages,
Each time between woman and man,
Each century unto the other,
Ere time and the ages began.

When drawn is the magickal circle,
By sword or athame of power,
It's compass between the two worlds lies,
In Land of the Shades for that hour.

This world has no right then to know it,
And world of beyond will tell naught,
The oldest of Gods are invoked there,
The Great Work of magick is wrought.

For two are the mystical pillars,
That stand at the gate of the shrine,
And two are the powers of nature,
The forms and the forces divine.

The dark and the light in succession,
The opposites each unto each,
Shown forth as a God and a Goddess:
Of this did our ancestors teach.

By night he's the wild wind's rider,
The Horn'd One, the Lord of the Shades.
By day he's the King of the Woodland,
The dweller in green forest glades.

She is youthful and old as she pleases,
She sails the torn clouds in her barque,
The bright silver Lady of midnight,
The crone who weaves spells in the dark.

The master and mistress of magick,
They dwell in the deeps of the mind,
Immortal and ever-renewing,
With power to free or to bind.

So drink the good wine to the old Gods,
And dance and make love in their praise,
Till Elphame's fair land shall receive us,
In peace at the end of our days.

And Do What You Will be the challenge,
So be it in love that harms none,
For this is the only commandment.
By magick of old be it done!

THE 13 GOALS OF A WITCH

According to Scott Cunningham

1. Know yourself

2. Know your Craft

3. Learn

4. Apply knowledge and wisdom

5. Achieve balance

6. Keep your words in good order

7. Keep your thoughts in good order

8. Celebrate life

9. Attune with the cycles of the Earth

10. Breath and eat correctly

11. Exercise the body

12. Meditate

13. Honor the Goddess and God

WICCAN THEOLOGY

THE FIVE ELEMENTS

Wiccan tradition states that there are five elements. It is through these elements and their constituents that all things are created, and made to exist. The elements are Air, Fire, Water, Earth, and Spirit. This assertion is not meant to be taken literally—they merely represent five forces or energies that are present in all things.

These five elements are also represented by the equilateral cross which. This is the keystone of the Wiccan altar and magick circle. Though the order and placement of the elements within this cross can be any way you like, the traditional placement is used here and is based on the four cardinal points of the compass.

The two heavy elements are Earth and Water, and are Passives. The two light elements are Air and Fire, and they are Actives. Earth is the opposite of Air, and Fire is the opposite of Water.

There are also five elements of the human individual, which are similarly not to be taken literally: the mind, the heart, the soul, the body, and the essence.
Each of these five human elements is related to the five basic elements. The significance and application of these

elements will become more evident as you learn about spellwork, auric work, and crystals.

PHILOSOPHY AND VARIATIONS IN THE TRADITIONS.

Wiccan views of divinity center around a Goddess and God. Some subgroups of Wiccans give the Goddess primacy over the God. Some Wiccans are polytheists or pantheists, while others say that 'All the Goddesses are one Goddess, and all the Gods one God'. Some see divinity as having a real, concrete and eternal existence; others see the Goddesses and Gods as archetypes or symbols, helpful for the purposes of visualization and connection.

Most sects of Wicca see the Goddess and the God as cyclical. The Goddess progresses from Maiden to Mother to Crone along with the seasons; the God from a youth to a young man to a sage. A belief consistent in most sects of Wicca is that the gods are able to manifest in personal form, either through dreams, as actual physical manifestations, or through the bodies and voices of Priestesses and Priests.

Gardnerian Wicca often refers to the God and Goddess as the Lady and the Lord. In this context, they are envisioned as primal cosmic figures, and sources of limitless power. According to Gerald Gardner the gods of Wicca are ancient gods of the British Isles: a Horned God of hunting, death and magic who rules over the after-world, and a goddess, the Great Mother, who gives regeneration and rebirth to souls of the dead and nurtures the living. Gardner refers to these gods as tribal, and compares them to the Gods of the Egyptians.

There are, of course, individual takes on the nature of the God and the Goddess, and the relationship between Wiccans and the God and Goddess can differ. Many have a kind of polytheistic view that the gods and goddesses of all cultures are aspects of the Lord or the Lady. Others feel that various Gods and Goddesses are distinct and not to be confused.

Some Wiccans, particularly in feminist or Dianic traditions, have a monotheistic belief in the Goddess. Still others see the Gods and Goddesses of personifications, and not absolutes. Some Wiccans conceive deities as akin to thoughtforms. A unified supreme god called the Prime Mover is also recognized by some groups, referred to by

Scott Cunningham as "The One" and Patricia Crowther as *Dryghten.*

For most Wiccans, the Lord and Lady are seen as polarities, or opposites, sometimes symbolized as the Sun and Moon. Some Wiccans refer to the God as the spark of life and inspiration within the Goddess, both her lover and her child. In some traditions, notably Feminist branches of Dianic Wicca, the Goddess is worshipped solely.

There is an element of pantheism in most Wiccan sects as well: since the Goddess is said to create, nurture, and contain all life within her, all beings are a piece of the divine. For some Wiccans, this idea also involves elements of animalism, and plants, rivers, rocks, and ritual tools are seen as spiritual entities, mere pieces of a total, living being.

WHEEL OF THE YEAR

WICCAN CELEBRATIONS

Wiccans celebrate 8 major rituals each year called "Sabbats". There are 4 major and 4 minor Sabbats. The major Sabbats include:

Imbolc (February 2nd),

Beltane (April 30th),

Lughnasadh (August 1st)

Samhain (October 31st),

while the minor Sabbats are:

Ostara (Spring Equinox, March 21st),

Litha (Summer Solstice, June 21st),

Madon (Autumn Equinox, September 21st),

Yule (Winter Solstice, December 21st).

The Sabbats are solar rituals marking the points of the sun's yearly cycle, and make up half of the Wiccan ritual year. The other half is made up with "Esbats", which are the Full Moon celebrations. There are 13 full moons each year which Wiccans take to symbolize the goddess.

A Sabbat, according to the church, is an assembly of witches that gather so as to renew vows to Satan. The word "sabbat" is a borrowed word, as it same root word as "sabbath", which is a biblical period of rest. Of course, witches and Wiccans in no way affirm loyalty to Satan. The Sabbats are solar festivals following the solar year, and so their mythology emphasizes the life cycle of the God. The God is associated with the sun, and the Goddess is associated with the moon.

The Sabbats' names and some of their purposes have been inspired by and taken from a variety of pagan holidays from a variety of cultures. The major Sabbats are loosely Celtic, while the minor Sabbats are Anglo, Saxon, and Norse. This may explain some of the duplication of significances between adjoining major and minor Sabbats.

Wiccans believe time is cyclical, and conceive the passing of time not in a line, but a circle. The circle is split into two halves for summer and winter, with the divisions occurring at Samhain and Beltaine. The two halves are ruled by a Light God and a Dark God, or by the Goddess and the God. The God rules winter, while the Goddess rules summer.

The Wheel, or circle, is composed of the four equinoxes and solstices as minor Sabbats, and the cross-quarter days as major Sabbats.

Those unfamiliar with Wicca will almost certainly notice the similarity between Wiccan and Christian holidays. This is because both religions were heavily influenced by the same pagan sources.

The Days referred to here begin strictly at midnight, and in the southern hemisphere, Sabbats are generally celebrated 6 months off from the traditional dates.

FOUR MAJOR SABBATS:

Samhain (sow' en)
15 degrees of Scorpio, or November 1
Wiccan mythology: The death of the God
Samhain is the Wiccan New Year and the Feast of the Dead. It serves to commemorate the dead, particularly those who have passed away recently, or who are particularly missed. Samhain is also a time for reflecting upon the last year, making plans for the upcoming one, and assessing the progress made on last year's goals.

It is only somewhat accurate to say that we start the year off by celebrating death. Another way to look at it is to acknowledge that Death is necessary for rebirth.

The Goddess enters her Dark phase as she mourns her son and consort, and the Dark God takes up the rulership of Winter, leading the Wild Hunt of the Fey upon the earth.

Imbolc (im' molc) or (im' bolc)

15 degrees of Aquarius, or February 1

Wiccan mythology: Goddess recovers from childbirth, becomes Maiden.

Imbolc is the beginning of Spring. The God continues to mature, as can be witnessed in the lengthening days, and celebrations frequently serve to honor light. The Crone Goddess of Winter transforms to the Maiden, who prepares the earth to begin its growth cycle once more. Imbolc is therefore also a holiday of purification. It was inspired by an Irish holiday dedicated to Brigid or Bride, goddess of creativity, smithing, and healing.

Beltaine

15 degrees of Taurus, or May 1

Wiccan mythology: marriage of the Goddess and God

Beltaine, the start of Summer, is the most important Sabbat after Samhain. It is a celebration of joy and life. Named for the Celtic fire god Bel, the lighting of fires is a ceremonial part of Beltaine events.

On Beltaine, the Light God has matured to the age of rulership and takes over from the Dark God. The pregnant Goddess turns from Maiden to Mother.

Lughnasadh (loo' na sah) or (loon' sah)

15 degrees of Leo, or August 1

Wiccan mythology: Aging God

Lughnasadh is the beginning of Autumn and was the time of the first harvest, and so this is a holiday of preparation for the oncoming winter, an to remind us of the God's impending death. The Goddess also enters her phase as Crone. It is also a favorite time for handfasting or trial marriages

FOUR MINOR SABBATS:

Yule

Also know as Midwinter

Winter solstice (around December 22)

Wiccan mythology: The birth of the God

Yule is a celebration of life emerging from darkness and is honored with the exchange of presents. Evergreens, holly, ivy, wreaths, trees festooned with ornaments and decorations, and mistletoe can be symbolic of the God, still living and green in the dead of winter.

Eostara (os tar' a)

Vernal equinox (around March 22)

Wiccan mythology: Sexual union of the Goddess and God Eostara (which later changed into the word "Easter") is a celebration of fertility, conception and regeneration. It is also a triumph of light over dark as from now until Litha days will be longer than the nights. Eostara is a time for cultivating the growth of ideas and souls, caring for our bodies and making sure we haven't forgotten the goals stated at the New Year.

Litha

Also known as Midsummer

Summer solstice (around June 22)

Wiccan mythology: Apex of the God's life

This is holiday of transition, when the God transforms from young warrior to maturing sage. It is a time for rejoicing, but also of introspection, making sure plans are still on track and meditation.

Mabon

Autumnal equinox (around September 22)

Wiccan mythology: Decline of the God

Mabon was the second harvest, and is primarily a holiday of thanksgiving from the "fruits" of the Earth. It is also the day when the nights are longer than the days, and so it is a day of planning and reflection.

SPACE, ALTARS, TOOLS, CLOTHING AND NAMES

SPACE

Rituals and spells can be practiced anywhere: outdoors, in a special room or space in a house, in a shared area devoted solely to ritual work and magick. The space you choose should be one in which you feel safe. It should ideally be one where roommates or family members will not interfere with your altar or your tools, and will not be likely to interrupt or intrude.

You will want enough room, however, to be able to stand straight up with your arms spread all the way out. You should not feel crowded or cramped, or feel as though you can't move without knocking something over.

TOOLS

There is a special section on the wand, which is probably the tool most familiar to non-wiccans. Athames, chalices, cauldrons, censors, and mortars and pestles also come in very handy. Though most are used primarily as aids in visualization, their powers should not be underestimated.

Many Witches will find a knife, or athame, to be very useful for the commanding and manipulation of particularly strong energies. Appearance can vary, but in general, your athame should a double edged, dagger-like knife with a blade.

It can be used in place of a wand to cast a circle, or to symbolize the severing of bad energy. It should not be used for any purposes other than magickal workings, and to be treated with as much care as your wand.

Many witches also have a special cup for ceremonies and spells, called a chalice, though it can also come in the form of a cauldron, bowl, or goblet. It is used to contain water, wine, tinctures, potions, or other spell ingredients, and is usually made of brass, animal horn, crystal, glass or ceramic. In ritual the chalice can not only hold ingredients, but serve the purpose of representing the female where the athame represents the male.

As you begin to peruse spells and rituals, you will no doubt see that you will frequently need a cord. The cord is also known as the girdle, and can be used to measure the radius of circles, for binding things or people, or as a symbol.

The censer is used for burning incense during ritual in order to purify the ritual space or area. Many varieties and styles are available and all, from the most ornate to the simplest, are adequate. Incense can be purchased, or, ideally, made yourself. Though the censer can be quite adequate in setting mood, many find a bell to be even more useful. A gong or small bell can be used to signify the beginning of a spell, ritual, or ceremony.

You may also wish for a special knife or pestle for grinding and cutting herbs. These may not be for any use save magickal ritual or ingredient preparation.

All tools must be cleansed and consecrated before use in the same manner that the wand must be cleansed and consecrated. There is no need for separate rituals to consecrate each tool; all may be consecrated at once.

WAND MAKING AND CONSECRATION

As you progress in your studies, you will no doubt find use for a wand. A wand can be purchased or made. It can merely be a stick from a beloved backyard tree or it can be an expensive, ornately carved staff purchased from a Magick store.

Either way, make sure you know what the wand is made of. Know what kind of wood it is, and what properties that particular kind of tree has. Of course, some may disagree with me, but I am of the opinion that a wand is a very personal item, and do not need to be made out of wood. A wand can be made out of plastic, or out of a car antenna, for that matter. What matters is that you feel drawn to that particular piece of wood, metal, or plastic, and feel that it can effectively channel your energies and powers.

Once you have selected your wand, it will need to be cleansed, and charged. Select a spot that is special to you, preferably out doors. You will need dried sage to burn, a silver or porcelain bowl, and a white candle.

Light the candle and pick up the wand, and say:

> *"I have chosen this wand.*
> *It will assist me in my work."*

Visualize the wand being cleared of any negativity, especially if it been touched by others, or served another purpose. Continue till the wand feels clear to you. Now visualize positive energy flowing from you, down your arm, through your fingers, and into the wand to its very tip. Visualize strong waves of energy flowing through your body to the wand. Say:

> *"In the names of the Goddess and God*
> *(or Athena and Apollo, or whichever names you*
> *wish), I bless and make sacred this wand.*
> *I charge this wand by the element of Earth."*

Point the wand towards the North, saying:

> *"May the powers of the Earth cleanse and fill the*
> *wand I have chosen."*

Pass the wand through the smoke of the smoldering sage and say:

> *"In the names of the Goddess and God (use any names you wish), I bless and make sacred this wand, tool of my craft. I charge this wand by the element Air."*

Point the wand to the East, saying:

> *"May the powers of the Air cleanse and fill the wand I have chosen."*

Pass the wand through the candle flame, saying:

> *"In the names of the Goddess and God (using any names), I bless and make sacred this wand, tool of my craft. I charge this wand by the element Fire."*

Point the wand to the South, saying:

> *"May the powers of Fire cleanse and fill the wand I have chosen."*

Sprinkle the wand with water, saying:

> *"In the names of the Goddess and God (using any names), I bless and make sacred this wand, tool of my craft. I charge this wand by the element Water."*

Point the wand to the West, saying:

> *"May the powers of water cleanse and fill the wand I have chosen."*

> *"This wand is now ready, being consecrated and charged to assist me in my work. So mote it be."*

Perform other workings if you wish, then close the circle.

ALTARS

An altar is a space that honors the God and the Goddess. It can be a tiny corner of a closet sized apartment, or a giant wall of a spacious loft. The space you choose is up to you. As you develop a sense of your identity as a Wiccan, you may choose to arrange the altar in any way that pleases you. Until you figure out your own aesthetic preferences, and gain confidence in your skills in the craft, here is an example that can inspire and guide you.

Construction and Use of

First of all you need a space to name your altar. This can be erected and dissembled if you are a small space, or a shared space. You can take a simple table or chest and cover it with a pretty cloth to start. The color of the cloth is up to you.

Secondly an altar usually consists of four quarters; the North, East, South and West. Some witches physically divide their quarters with crystals, cords, or thread. All quarters are represented by a physical object. For example the North quarter can have a crystal, or a dish holding sand, whilst the South can hold a bundle of dried sage or a candle. It is up to you to figure out which direction has more male or female energy, and to find an appropriate representation.

The West is dedicated to water and can have a chalice or bowl of water. Earth where you to turn when craving stability and money, the East holds wisdom, the South gives of passion and creativity and the West for emotion and raw energies. It is entirely up to you to select appropriate representations of each quarter.

A very important part of your altar is the middle. This represents the Threefold Goddess and can be represented by a kettle, a fertility statuette, or a silver bowl for brewing potions and mixing herbs. If this doesn't appeal to you, you can put a special or cherished object in the middle. A cherished locket or stuffed animal can even serve as the middle point of the altar. Anything that has meaning to you will suffice.

Another important thing are your God and Goddess familiars—for instance, do you relate more to Athena or Diana? Apollo or Thor? If you have not latched on to a specific deity you can place a white candle as your Goddess and a black one as your God, or statuettes, or really anything that connects you to them. A conch, a crystal, a figurine, or pendants will do just fine.

The altar can be decorated according to the seasons and Sabbats. In the autumn, you can scatter nuts or dried fruits on your altar. In the winter, for example, you can put pine needles in the center bowl. There are a multitude of ways to pay honor to the seasons and Sabbats and this is entirely up to you.

Should an unfortunate accident befall your altar (for example at the hands of a curious child or a rambunctious pet) do not despair. Merely re-consecrate the space and recreate it to your liking.

Basic Altar Setup

As mentioned previously, the most common altar tools are the Goddess and God candles, incense, an altar plate, an athame and a chalice. Some altars also include quarter candles.

Here is an example of an altar layout that puts the four Elements at your fingertips

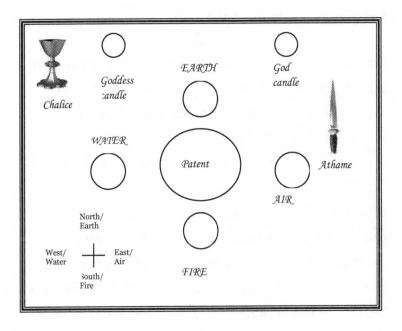

The chalice and athame are located in appropriate alignment with the Goddess and God candles.

The Goddess and God candles are set to the rear of the altar with nothing behind them. This is ideal because you never have to reach over their candles and endanger catching your robe or sleeves on fire.

Please keep in mind that this is a basic setup. If you use other items during your ritual such as crystals, candles, food, etc., try to keep them placed with the appropriate element or direction.

CHOOSING A WICCAN NAME

One of the first things you may want to do when you start exploring your identity as a Wiccan is to select your new name. Using a name that represents you and your relationship with the Goddess and God also is a reminder to direct your life down the new path you have chosen.

Not all people who become Pagans or enter the Craft do change their names or add to them—it is recommended, though optional. Once you have made the decision that you'd like to, you can start narrowing down your choices a bit. Do you want a name that exemplifies your present personality and strengths? Or a name that captures all you aspire to be? What kind of magick do you perform? What is your personality like?

Your name can be a noun, the proper name of one of the Goddesses of Gods, or a made up word. It can be Demeter, the Goddess of the Harvest, or Tiger Lilly, the name of a beautiful flower.

Some witches choose Earth names. I have met Witches named Willow, Ash, Thorn, and Mud. Many male Wiccans choose to name themselves after animals, such as Deer, Tiger, or Coyote. And of course, there are the new-agey universe names, such as Starsong, Moonsong, Moonmist, and Zephyr.

Take all the time needed to decide as it can confuse people—and yourself when you make a name change. This especially applies to networking when you are in contact with many other Wiccans, particularly online when a name change can be a pain as well as confusing.

Most pagans do not legally change their names, and use them in the Circle, with other pagans, and as proof of authorship of creative endeavors such as books, stories, paintings, glassblowing, and sculpting.

Remember that a name is not only what you are now, but what you want to be, but don't go overboard. Keep in mind that others of the Craft will be addressing you and you might feel ridiculous if someone one day greets you as Queen Mother Goddess the Ultimate Ruler of the Entire Universe, or something.

There are no wrong names or wrong answers, however, so long as you select something that is meaningful to you, and will inspire you in your work.

RITUALS

WHAT IS A RITUAL?

A ritual is a formalized procedure that serves to bond a coven together, or for an individual Wiccan to express devotion to the God or Goddess. Wiccan rituals can be performed alone, or with others. They can be led by a priest or priestess, but this is not necessarily mandatory. Usually a ritual will commemorate an important event, such as one of the Sabbats, or the birth of a child. Sometimes rituals are performed merely to honor the Lord and the Lady, and to allow the practitioner to experience a connection with either or both of them.

WHY HAVE RITUALS?

Wiccan rituals serve the same purpose as a ritual in any other religion. They can provide a framework for a common experience among devotees. Or they can serve to remind practitioners of the nature of their relationship to each other, and to the Goddess and God.

CONSTRUCTION/DESIGN OF RITUALS

Every ritual is different, but there are some generalizations that can be made as to the different components of the average Wiccan ritual.

Most Wiccan rituals begin by "casting the circle", which is the act of defining sacred space. The magic circle, within Wicca, is regarded as a boundary between the outside world and the sacred world within. The magic circle is also considered a receptacle for power, and acts to protect the practitioner from distractions or interference. Usually the circle is cast using a sword, though any of the "masculine" tools, like the athame, wand, or staff can be used instead.

You will learn more about how exactly to cast a magic circle in a later section. Next, if the ritual is taking place in a group, the leader may choose to anoint each person with oil, sprinkle person with water, smudge each person with incense, or offer each person a token to bless them and welcome them into the sacred space.

Next is the sweeping of the circle. This will rid the circle of unwanted energies and influences. It is done by sweeping the circle once around with a witches broom. Some may also choose to burn incense or sprinkle some water on the space.

Once the circle has been swept, the elemental powers will be called.

Here is an example of traditional Quarter Calls...

All raise will their athames and face East, with the Priestess in front. She holds the Pentacle in the air and they say:

> *Lords of the Watchtowers of the East, Lords of Air, I call you to witness our rites and to protect our circle.*

This is done for each quarter of the circle until all elements have been drawn from their corresponding directions.

Next, the leader of the ritual Draws Down the Moon. This means that the Goddess is being invited into the circle. The spirit of the Goddess enters the priestess, to speak with her voice. The priest, if there is one, will call the Goddess. He might say:

> *I invoke thee and call upon thee, O Lady of us all, bearer of all fruit, I invoke thee to descend upon*

the body and voice of this thy servant and
priestess.

Something similar is then recited by the priestess to Draw Down the Sun. Some traditions prefer not to do a full Drawing Down for every occasion, but instead make a Call to the deities to be invited to be present spiritually. There are not exact scripts for the calls, though they usually follow a format like the one above.

TOOLS OF RITUALS

ROBES:

Some witches feel that the best way to do ritual work is to be sky-clad, or naked. At times, this is just not feasible. And even when it is possible, some of us feel more comfortable clothed. If you are uncomfortable, or feeling vulnerable, your spellwork will suffer, hence you may want ritual robes.

There is no strict pattern or design for ritual robes. You may have a different set of robes for each season, or even each Sabbat. Some Witches feel that whatever you wear for ritual should only be for the ritual. Wearing the clothing or jewelry at other times will take away the power of the garments at other times.

Obviously, we get naked when it's NOT ritual time, so even if you're opting to be sky-clad, you will want a special necklace or bracelet that will make Rituals special. Some feel that having special clothing and jewelry for rituals makes them charged with more energy; others feel that putting them on triggers more focus and an improved mental state.

If working in a coven, there may be a "dress code" to make sure that the rituals and rites are treated with respect, but you will most likely have plenty of freedom in designing the clothing you wear.

THE BATH

Before performing spellwork, concocting a potion, or even engaging in deep meditation, it is necessary to take a ritual bath. Those that wish to practice in a coven will be expected to have taken a ritual bath before appearing for initiation and other important ceremonies.

You will need:
A small silver or porcelain bowl with spring water
Sea salt
A white candle
Incense of your choice
Oils or herbs of your choice.

Select a time and place where you know that you will be undisturbed. Lock the door and turn off the phone, if need be. Draw a hot bath and add some essence, oils, or herbs. Figure out which herbs will benefit you the most. For example, merely wishing to cleanse and purify, sage might be a good choice. If about to perform a love charm, rose oil might be better.

Turn off all the lights and light a single white taper. The white taper should be unused, and should have a candle holder that will allow you to put it down and not worry about it. A simple votive candle will do if no taper is available.

Light a stick of incense or place some on a glowing coal in a censer that you can pick up, and sprinkle a pinch of sea salt in a white dish or silver bowl.

Once the bath is drawn and any oils have been added to it as desired, take the candle and make three slow passes over the water. Say:

> *"By this fire I purify this bathwater. May all impurities, contaminants, and evil energies flee before its light."*

Set the candle down, making sure it's somewhere where it can flicker freely without worry of setting anything on fire or being knocked over. Sprinkle the sea salt in the bathwater and Say:

> *"With this I purify this ritual bath. May all impurities, contaminants, and evil energies flee from it.*

Set down the dish and pick up the incense, or, if you wish, bundle of smoldering sage. Say:

> *"By this smoke I purify this ritual bath. May my good energy and aspirations be carried in the smoke to the Lady.*

Set down the incense. Pour the water into the bath. It can be spring water, rain water, or ocean water. Say:

> *"By this I purify this ritual bath. May this bath contain the Waters of Life that spring from Mother Earth."*

Undress and enter your bath. Enjoy it for as long as you want. Use this time to meditate on that which you wish to accomplish. Dry off with a freshly cleaned towel that has been allowed to line dry outside if at all possible. The color of the towel can be coordinated with the work you intend to do.

Anoint yourself with whatever oils you plan to use. Dress in ritual robes or other clothing if you must drive or walk to the site where you will be working the craft.

There will be times when the full ritual bath is not feasible. You may cleanse and consecrate special water and keep it in a bottle for emergencies. Though not ideal, it will be sufficient in an emergency.

CASTING A CIRCLE

In many spells, the first action is often to cast a circle. Few spells explain how as it is a basic skill that every Wiccan knows. Though simple, it is a crucial step in performing any work.

Before you even think about casting a circle, you need to know why and what you'll be doing with it. Think about exactly what you are going to do, the reasons behind your spell, what resources you will need, and what you hope to achieve from the spell.

The first step in casting a circle, or indeed beginning most spells, is to cleanse and ground yourself. Take a ritual bath, and if it is not possible to be sky clad, then dress in ritual robes.

Once you yourself are clean, you must clean the area in which you will be doing your work. If you are working indoors, sweep, vacuum, or just tidy up in general. If outdoors, clear any litter from your space. Then, close your eyes and concentrate until you feel centered. Once this is done, open your eyes. Point your wand at the circle and then and then visualize fire coming from your wand and burning away all negativity and impurities. You may instead visualize wind sweeping through the space and carrying bad energies away.

Once the area is cleansed, mark the area. Traditionally the Circle should consist of 3 concentric circles, each 6" apart in radius, with the Pentacle inscribed inside the smaller circle, facing North. If this is impossible, just work with whatever space is available. If indoors, you could mark its boundaries with Tarot Cards, Crystals, herbs, Chalk, charcoal, or even a magic marker. If outdoors, leaves and twigs will do.

Then, scatter a pinch of salt and walk the boundary. Say:

> *'I call upon you*
> *To protect and consecrate this Circle,*
> *May this ground be pure and clean,*
> *Free from negativity!'*

Next walk around again, but this time with water (preferably rainwater, spring water, or ocean water) saying,

> *'I call upon you*
> *To protect and consecrate this Circle,*
> *May this ground be safe and pure and clean,*
> *Free from negativity!'*

Lastly repeat with burning incense or sage:

> *'I call upon you,*
> *To protect and consecrate this Circle,*
> *May this ground be pure and clean,*
> *Free from negativity!'*

Then set out your Altar and any materials you will need to work your spell. Remember that once you've cast your circle, you may not leave its boundaries (or break the circle) until your Ritual is ended, so make sure you have everything with you. In the event that you have forgotten something that you need, or the wind has blown it out of the circle, you may cut a door into the circle and exit to retrieve whatever it is you need.

Now, you are ready to do your work.

INITIATION

Although this book is primarily geared to those who will be practicing Wicca alone, I have included this section on initiation into a coven so that the new Wiccan will know what to expect should she or he be invited to one. If a coven does invite you to come to a meeting, this is not a guarantee of membership. It is a chance for you to figure out if that particular coven is the right place for you, and for the coven to figure out if you are right for them. When you do meet the coven, they will try to ascertain whether or not your personality will compliment the personalities of existing members. They will want to see that you have read widely on the subject, and are patient enough to go through a waiting period, usually a year and a day, among others.

Most witches are cautious, particularly those living in a community where their way of life will be met with prejudice and suspicion. As for you, seek out a coven which will match your lifestyle and character.

Although some covens wear robes, the traditional way of working in the Circle is to be sky-clad (naked). The first initiation is virtually an introduction to a new way of life. You are made a 'Child of the Goddess'; you are shown the tools of the Craft; told the ways of working magic, and asked to swear to keep the secrets of the Art. This is called the First Degree.

The Second Degree is the second and final stage of the initiation. The ritual symbolizes that you have been re-born with the new magical personality. A new name is given to you, and from then on, you will be known by that name when working in the Circle.

A way will be shown, and knowledge shared, yet the journey is always 'alone' and the true 'will' tested to the very brink of breaking point.

Initiations into witch circles are fairly flexible. Different covens may have slightly different invocations or approaches. However, the old idea that initiation must pass from the male to the female, and from the female to the male, still is an important part of most, if not all, initiations. A male must be initiated by a woman, and a female by a man. There is one exception: a woman may initiate her daughter and a man may initiate his son.

Though initiation ceremonies can vary, there are a few central concepts that are consistent. The initiate must pledge whole-hearted acceptance of the witch religion, and an oath of loyalty, were the main features. The new initiate-also called a novice—is given a new name. It is with this new name that he or she will forever be addressed when working with the coven.

Some covens still require initiates to renounce whatever faith it is they held prior—Christianity, Judaism, Islam, whatever—but this is rare.

After the oath of allegiance and affirmation of belief, the novice is marked with oil, wine, or charcoal.

Sample Initiation Ceremonies:

Here are two examples of different initiation ceremonies used by actual covens. They will help you get an idea of what to expect.

Priestess: Hear the words of the Threefold Goddess! Whenever you have need of anything, you shall assemble in some secret place and adore me, the Threefold Goddess, Maiden, Mother, and Crone. She who would learn all sorcery yet has not won its deepest secrets, them I will teach her, in truth, all things as yet unknown. Sing, feast, dance, make music and love in My presence, for Mine is the ecstasy of the spirit and Mine also is joy on earth. For

My law is love unto all beings. Nor do I demand sacrifice, for behold, I am the mother of all things."

Processional

The Initiate is left to meditate as the others rise and follow the High Priest/ess into the Circle area and three times around, chanting:

"We all come from the Goddess,
And to her we shall return
Like a drop of rain,
Flowing to the ocean." (repeat)
Raising of the Circle

HIGH PRIEST/ESS takes the Sword from the altar and traces a circle around the group. When he/she returns to the north, he/she kneels and salutes saying: "Hail and welcome, frosty Spirits of the North. Lend to us your power and protection this night that <Initiate's born name> may be given a true initiation to justly wield the power of Earth. So mote it be!"

ALL (envisioning a wall of dark green light springing up from the circle): "So mote it be!"

HIGH PRIEST/ESS advances to the east, kneels and salutes saying: "Hail and welcome, bright Spirits of the East. Lend to us your power and protection that <Initiate's born name> may be given a true initiation to justly wield the power of Air. So mote it be!"

ALL (envisioning a wall of lemon yellow light springing up from the circle, within the wall of green): "So mote it be!"

HIGH PRIEST/ESS advances to the south, kneels and salutes saying: "Hail and welcome, fiery Spirits of the South. Lend to us your power and protection that <Initiate's born name> may be given a true initiation to justly wield the power of Fire. So mote it be!"

ALL (envisioning a wall of crimson light springing up from the circle, within the walls of green and yellow): "So mote it be!"

HIGH PRIEST/ESS advances to the west, kneels and salutes saying: "Hail and welcome, tireless Spirits of the West. Lend to us your power and protection that <Initiate's born name> may be given a true initiation to justly wield the power of Water. So mote it be!"

ALL (envisioning a wall of dark blue light springing up from the circle, within the walls of green, yellow and red): "So mote it be!"
Statement of Purpose

HIGH PRIEST/ESS: "I call upon the Horned God; I call upon the Maiden, the Mother and the Crone; I call upon the Spirits of Earth, Air, Fire and Water; I call upon the Hosts of the Mighty Dead; and I call every true Witch within this circle to witness that we are here to consecrate <Initiate's name> as Priest(ess) and Witch. The circle is cast!"

ALL (envisioning the walls of the circle bending together overhead and flowing together under the floor to form a hemisphere of bright white light): "So mote it be!"
The Warning

HIGH PRIEST/ESS cuts a gate in the circle and roughly leads the Initiate to kneel at the edge before the gate, then balances the sword-point over the Initiate's heart (the Initiate raises hir hands to support the point). "You stand at the edge of a place that is between the worlds, in the presence of the Gods and under the watchful eye of the Mighty Dead. If you go any further, you embark on a path that cannot be safely turned aside before your death. Feel the sharpness of the blade at your breast, and know this in your heart that it would be better for you to throw yourself forward and spill out your life than to enter this circle with fear or falseness in your heart."

INITIATE: "I come with perfect love and perfect trust."

HIGH PRIEST/ESS lays down the sword, lifts the Initiate to his or her feet and kisses him or her. "Thus are all first brought into the Circle.", then leads the Initiate to the altar and taking up the sword, re-draws the circle over the gateway.
Administration of the Oaths

HIGH PRIEST/ESS: "Blessed are your feet, that have brought you to this place. Blessed are your knees, that shall kneel at the altars of the Gods. Blessed is your sex, without which we could not be. Blessed is your breast, formed in strength and beauty. Blessed are your lips which shall speak the Words of Truth. Are you prepared to take the oath?"

INITIATE: "I am."

HIGH PRIEST/ESS: "Then kneel." (takes the Initiate's measure.) "You who have from birth been called <born name> but now seek to become <Craft name> -- do you willingly pledge yourself to the God and the Goddess?"

INITIATE: So mote it be."

HIGH PRIEST/ESS: "And do you swear to keep silent all those things that must be kept silent and to respect that which is taught to you?"

INITIATE: "I willingly swear to keep silent all that must be kept silent and to respect that which is taught to me. So mote it be."

HIGH PRIEST/ESS: "And by what surety do you swear all of these things?"

INITIATE: "All of these things I do swear, by my mother's womb and my hope of future lives, knowing well that my Measure has been taken in the presence of the Mighty Ones. Should I fail utterly in my oaths, may my powers desert me, and may my own tools turn against me. So mote it be. So mote it be. So mote it be!

ALL yell quickly: "SO MOTE IT BE!"
Triggering of the Spell

ALL grab the Initiate quickly and hoist her into the air (if possible), chanting the Initiate's new name over and over again, and carry him or her three times quickly around the circle. When they return to the starting point, they set him or her down face-down and touch her or him in a gentle massage. Through all of this they continue chanting the Initiate's new name, falling off in volume and speed as the pressure relaxes.

HIGH PRIEST/ESS: "Know that the hands that have touched you are the hands of love. (removes initiate's blindfold)

HIGH PRIEST/ESS hands the sword to the Initiate and leads her the East, where they both kneel. "Behold, restless Spirits of Water -- I bring before you <new name>, who has been consecrated as Priest/ess and Witch!" Repeats at the South, West, and finally North.

ALL (including High Priest/ess and Initiate) join hands in the Circle.

HIGH PRIEST/ESS: "Thank you Spirits of the Mighty Dead, Spirits of the Four Elements, and awesome Lord and Lady for hallowing our circle. Go or stay as you will -- our circle is ended."

ALL ground and center, then absorb the power of the Circle and return it to the Earth beneath their feet.

HIGH PRIEST/ESS (after a suitable pause): "Our lovely rite draws to its end. Merry meet, merry part, and merry meet again. Blessed Be!"

ALL: "BLESSED BE!"

SAMPLE INITATION BY A PRIEST AT THE FULL MOON

PRIEST: "This is the time of Full Moon, a time for rekindling of light. The struggle for higher light is: That we may see it, and seeing it, work and live by it. We are about to embark upon a solemn ceremony to rekindle the light of Knowledge, the light of Will, the light of Compassion, the light of Steadfastness; we will combine these lights, and rekindle the light of Dedication in our Sister (Brother) here before us.

_____, here have you been taught the ways
of the Wise, that you might count yourself among those
who serve the Gods, among the brothers and sisters of the
Wicca, those who are called the shapers of the universe."

PRIEST: "I now direct your attention to the two lights upon
our altar, the one representing the Sun, the God, and the
High Priest; the other representing the Moon, the Goddess,
and the High Priestess. The High Priest and Priestess,
presiding over the coven, may be thought of as 'One light to
rule the day, one light to rule the night'. Since these lights
are both beneficent, each having honor in its place, the
Craft of the Wise does not set day against night, God
against Goddess, Priest against Priestess. In the Craft, we
do not define evil as a negative power, rather as the lack of
light; where there is the light of Sun or Moon, God or
Goddess, there can be no lack of light. Choose one, or both;
place light within yourself, and nurture it."

"In times past, the Circle of Initiation was called a
'Hermetic Circle', after Hermes, the ancient name for the
planet Mercury." In astrology, the house of the Sun is in
the zodiacal sign of the lion, which is the fifth house; the
house of the Moon is in Cancer, the crab, and is in the
fourth house; and the day house of the planet Mercury is in
the Gemini, the Twins, and is the third house. These
numbers, three, four and five, were sacred to many ancient

peoples, as the dimensions of the Pythagorean Triangle, in which the square of five, twenty five, is equal to the sum of the squares of four and three, or sixteen and nine. Knowledge of this triangle was essential to builders; you are also a builder-you are building your character."

PRIESTESS: "I now direct your attention to the several lights surrounding us, in the East, South, West, and North. Let us now examine these lights, and see what we can discern within them of human character."
"In the building of character, the Eastern light is denoted the Lamp of Beauty, and stands for accomplishments; for learning, skill in art, poetry, in song and instrumental music, in painting and sculpture. It exemplifies the art of making one's self attractive to those about one. It is an old saying that 'Beauty is as Beauty does'. It causes great distress to see these noble graces of character prostituted to ignoble ends. Remember well the lesson of the Lamp of Beauty and accept the blessing of the East."

Initiate is censed with incense from the censer which has been previously placed in the East.

PRIEST: "The light in the South is denoted the Lamp of Life, and stands for individuality, and for energy; for fervency, for zeal and vitality. It exemplifies passions, desires and appetites. It means loves and hates, sympathies and abhorrence's, and what is more than all the rest of these, it means heart and joy in the work of life. Remember well the lesson of the Lamp of Life and accept the blessing of the South."

Initiate is circled three times with the brazier, previously placed in the South.

PRIESTESS: "Look now to the West, and observe the Lamp of Compassion, which stands for 'fellow-feeling'. Every work in life demands a price. Labor, tears, self-denial, self-recrimination, the very blood of life is sometimes the price of a truly great work. Look to your fellow travelers on the road; note with care what sacrifice they have made in their progress toward the truth; allow them their faults, commiserate with them in their failures and rejoice with them when they succeed. Remember well the lesson of the Lamp of Compassion and accept the blessing of the West."

Initiate is circled three times with water and his/her hands washed in a laving bowl, previously placed in the West.

PRIEST: "Look now to the North, and observe the lamp of obedience. The laws of the Gods are inevitable, and the more we, as children of the Gods, understand and work in accordance with them, the greater is the sum of our happiness. Obedience in character means order, the subjection to one's principles, the fear to do wrong, and the desire to learn and do right. Many would rather give charity than do justice. They swell with emotion, weep with sentiment, howl with the mob, so long as their own particular little tyranny or injustice is not touched. The Lamp of Obedience exemplifies firm will and determination of character, in spite of difficulties, dangers and losses. So also the Lamp of Obedience stands for self-control, perseverance and prudence. In time of peace, prepare for war; when shines the sun, expect the cloud; and in darkness wait patiently for the coming light. 'When all the sky is draped in black and beaten by tempestuous gales, and the shuddering ship seems all awreck, calmly trim once more the tattered sail, repair the broken rudder and set again for the old determined course.' Remember well the lesson of the Lamp of Obedience and accept now the blessing of the North."

Initiate's hands are marked with damp earth from a bowl in the North. Initiate is then led back south of the altar.

PRIESTESS: "Of the character thus illuminated and thus guided by the lights here on the altar, and by the Lamps of Beauty, Life, Compassion and Obedience, it may be said, 'Though the world perish and fall away, he/she remains.'"

Initiate then takes the Oath/Obligation, kneeling.

"In the names of Arianhrod and Bran; Diana and Appolyon; Heartha and Cernunnos; and by the powers of Earth, Air, Fire and Water, I, _____, pledge to love, worship and honor the Goddess in her many aspects; and her Consort, the Horned One, Lord of Death and Ruler of Chaos; to always be true to the Art and its secrets; to never abuse the Art or my own powers; and to keep this pledge always in my heart, in my mind, in my body and in my spirit. This I pledge, by the Circle of Life, by Cerridwen's Sacred Cauldron and by my own hopes of a future life."

Initiate stands. High Priestess places a necklace over Initiate's head.

PRIESTESS: "The Circle is a place between the worlds and outside time. The Circle is also the Symbol of Life, Death and Rebirth. We wear the necklace as a token of the Sacred Circle and as a sign that we are part of all it symbolizes."

High Priest strikes the bell three times.

PRIEST: "Hear ye, Lady of Life and Lord of Death! Hear ye, Ancient Guardians of the Powers of Air, Fire, Water and Earth! In this place, by our hands and will, _____, known to us as _____, has been duly pledged and anointed a Priest/ess of the Second Degree!"

MEDITATIONS

GUIDED MEDITATION

"Meditation" describes a state of purposeful, often self-induced, state of concentration. Sometimes, the purpose of meditation involves the pursuit of completely clearing the mind; other times it focuses on a specific object of thought or awareness. It usually involves turning the attention inward to a single point of reference. Meditation has been practiced in the East for thousands of years. The word "meditation" in the West has come to describe a wide variety of spiritual activities that emphasize stillness, concentration, or heightened self awareness.

Though meditation can be practiced alone, some prefer to engage in a practice referred to as "guided" meditation. In this practice, a priestess, priest, guru, teacher, spiritual authority, or spiritual leader guides the subject into a state of self-awareness and deep relaxation. The meditation leader may begin by asking the subject, or subjects, to bring awareness to the physical body to scan for any tension. The subjects will usually be asked to do this with their eyes closed. Next, the leader will lead the subjects through a series of visualizations. The intention is to get the subjects to focus on the task at hand, and strive for stillness and self-awareness.

Some consider a yoga class, for example, to be a form of guided meditation, in which the teacher takes the class through a series of movements to bring peace, comfort, and alignment to the physical body. Doing so will free the spiritual body and mind of earthly distractions, and liberate the subject for deep relaxation.

Meditation can also be guided with the help of a CD or audio recording. Guided meditation is not just for beginners. There are experienced practitioners of meditation who prefer to be guided so as to liberate themselves from the work of maintaining focus, or thinking of a path of visualization. There are meditation classes offered at community colleges, yoga centers, or even on line or via packages of CDs. It is not necessary to start meditating in a guided setting, but may be useful for the beginner so he or she will know what the goal is, and what sorts of challenges to expect.

Ultimately, the goal of meditation is to free the mind from clutter and achieve absolute stillness of the mind. This will allow the self to become open to experiencing the collective unconscious, and exist in a state of pure and total awareness.

A Reference Guide for the Novice Wiccan

NONGUIDED MEDITATION

Non-guided meditation is exactly as it sounds. It is the practice of meditating without the aid of a teacher or guide. It is generally a solitary activity done in a sacred or specially designated space.

Some devote a certain amount of time each day to silent meditation. This is a good practice as it will help calm and relax the physical body and the mind. The excused used by many is that they "don't have time" for meditation.

This is, in my opinion, because they do not make time for it. Few are so busy that they do not have fifteen minutes per day to spare. Sitting still for as little as fifteen minutes in silent reflection will benefit the body, mind, and spirit. The positive impact on the rest of the day will be immeasurable.

Initially, I was reluctant to make time for meditation. It seemed like a waste of time to just sit or lie down and not "do" anything. Little did I know that meditation is far from doing "nothing." Learning the art of meditation takes perseverance, patience, and practice. It is not as easy as one might think to still the mind and clear it of all distractions for as little as five minutes, let alone fifteen minutes or an hour.

TECHNIQUES

There are endless techniques to meditation. If you choose to engage in guided meditation, the leader will usually take you through a process in which you first examine your physical body in a quest to relax and let go of all tension. You will then usually be asked to visualize yourself somewhere peaceful and free of worry, such as a beach or a place where you feel particularly safe.

One easy technique to try merely involves sitting down, relaxing the body, and focusing on the breath. The breath is usually a fairly important component of all forms of meditation. Breathing should be rhythmic and deep, but not so deep as to mimic hyperventilation. After you feel relaxed, take the point of view of a visitor to your mind. Watch your thoughts. Observe them calmly, without directing them or being directed by them. Whenever you find yourself deviating from the meditation and thinking about something else, gently bring your mind back to meditation.

Another technique is to repeat the same word, or few words over and over again in a "mantra". "Om" is an example of a mantra.

Some believe that the key to meditation is to focus on a mantra, or even on an object, until it is the only thought in the mind. The next step is to remove the mantra or object, to make the mind totally blank.

Others believe that part of meditation is engaging in self analysis and philosophizing, thinking of the essence of the self. Asking yourself "who am I?" for example and answering the question nonverbally, with an intuitive knowledge. A tangle of logic can follow this. If you say "I am observing my mind and consciousness", then you must ask yourself who is this observer. Is it you, or are the thoughts you? The mind can be observed, but not the self. When you observe the mind, you and the mind are both you. The general goal of meditation is to merge your mind and your inner narrator.

This is, admittedly, somewhat confusing and mind-boggling. However, it is not merely a game of semantics. The ultimate goal of meditation is to just Be, and erase the idle chatter of the mind.

It sounds simple enough to just sit around and relax. Really reaching that state of awareness and stillness, however, can take a lifetime to master.

GROUNDING/CENTERING

Learning how to "ground" and "center" is a very important set of skills to learn when working with energy. It is second in importance only to learning how to meditate and visualize. Though these four skills don't sound as exciting as, say, spellwork, they are the keystones of energy working and power.

Your physical center refers to the point within you where your weight is equally distributed. Your energy center is also a physical, but invisible, point in your body.

Much like your physical center of gravity, your center of energy can get out of balance. The feeling that results from this, however, is more subtle than the feeling that results from being physically off balance. When your energy center is "off balance", you may feel anxious, stressed, or disconnected. We "center" ourselves by sinking down into this energy center, becoming aware of the flow of our internal energies, and seeking to calm and steady them.

Once you've learned how to find your center, you can move on to grounding yourself. When an energy worker grounds, he or she focuses and expels his or her excess energy into the ground or earth. The most common way to do this is by sitting down—usually in lotus position or cross-legged--and letting extra energy seep out of the bottom of your spine. You can visualize yourself growing roots into the ground to carry this energy away. You can also visualize energy grounding out of you through your feet, if you're standing.

Grounding can allow you to shed extra energy and tension before beginning magick or energy work. Second, it allows you to let any excess energies raised during your working to seep out of you and in to the earth or ambient environment. After a particularly intense working, you may want to lay down and visualize the extra energy leaving your body.

PATHWORKING

Pathworking is the art of developing psychic awareness through creative visualization. "Visualization" is actually just a big word for "pretend" or "make believe". Giving an image to our impressions and thoughts can help us in our quest for awareness. Pathworking can be conducted alone, or with a priest/ess or leader to guide the group or practitioner.

The most novice of Wiccans can engage in Pathworking, and though it is possible to start alone, it is recommended that you find a group or a leader at first so you can get the hang of it.

TOTEMS

A totem is any entity, usually an animal, which watches over, protects, or assists a group or individual.

Although the term "totem" is of Ojibwa origin, Native Americans are not the only groups that believe in totemism. Similar beliefs have been found in Western Europe, Eastern Europe, Africa, Australia and the Arctic.

Your totem animal can be found through meditation. Enter a relaxed, meditative state. Picture yourself walking down a path to a cave. You step into the cave and see if your totem animal has chosen you. It will come to you and choose you; you do not choose the animal. Sometimes, a totem animal will come to you in your dream. Sometimes it takes months or even years for a totem animal to choose you.

When one has chosen you, you must not reject it because it's not "cool" enough. You may want a tiger, but see a mouse once you have entered the cave. Rejecting the mouse will make him angry, and understandably so! There is a reason Mouse chose you. Instead of discarding him, you must learn why, and what it says about you.

Totem animals are more a part of eclectic Wicca and general New Age-ism than Dianic or Gardnerian Wicca. Many, however, take a great amount of solace and comfort from their totem animals, as well as a great amount of power.

SHIELDING

Shielding is a technique for creating a magical 'force field' around you or your place of practice to act as protection from unwanted energy. There are different ways to do this, but one is to envision a web of energy around the area to be shielded. Unlike the circle you cast when beginning a ritual or spell, the energy field is a 3 dimensional sphere. It is powered by your physical energy, so being tired, under the influence, or un-grounded may affect your ability to effectively shield.

Warding is a similar technique. A Ward is a Shield anchored to a physical place, powered by Earth energy instead of your own physical energy. This has the advantage of leaving more energy for spell work. Reinforce the visualization regularly, and it can be a permanent shield to protect your Circle or home.

ASTRAL PROJECTION

Astral projection is the ability to send the soul to a place where the body is not. The body will appear to be sleeping while the soul floats. Below is a very effective method of achieving the meditative state necessary to astrally project. This is an extremely difficult task, so don't be discouraged if it is not possible right away. Some attempt for years before they are able to successfully astrally project!

Astral projection is not, as you might think, the ability to spy on others with your soul-self, or quickly pop over to Paris to check out the Metro. It is a deep meditative state in which you lose self awareness. When in this state, it is as though time is standing still. No external noise or disturbance can reach you. It takes much practice so be patient!

One of the chief barriers people learning to project face is impatience. Many people, used to a world of one hour dry cleaners and two minute microwaveable dinners, simply cannot sit still and focus for long enough. Learn the art of staying still before you attempt astral projection.

Step One: Relax

This includes both physical and mental relaxation. Before you begin, however, remove all jewelry and clothing. Darken the room so that no light can be seen through your eyelids. Lie down with your body along a north-south axis, with your head pointed northward. Be sure you are in a location where, and at a time when, there will be absolutely no noise to disturb you. Enter a state of relaxation Start perhaps by meditating, visualizing a pleasant place, or counting deep breaths. Then let go until you are hanging on to consciousness by a mere thread.

Step Two: Deepen This State

Begin to clear your mind. Look at the back of your eyelids until you notice patterns of color and light. Stare at them until they melt away. Relax even further until you cannot feel your body against the ground or the air on your skin.

Step Three: Heavy Limbs

Make your limbs become heavy. Listen to your heartbeat.

Step Four: Enter a state of Vibration.

This can be experienced as a mild tingling, or as is electricity is being shot through the body as your astral body tries to leave the physical one.

Step Five: Assert Control

Push the vibrations from your head to your feet, and then feel them surge back up again. Do this several times until you are sure you have 100% control. Give yourself the order that you will remember all that occurs. Breathe through your nose and concentrate on the void in front of you. Select a point a foot away from your forehead, then six feet. Focus there and reach out for the vibrations at that point and bring them back into your body.

Step Six: Initiate the Separation.

Don't let your concentration waver! Stay completely focused! Visualize your shadow self rising from your body part way, then returning.

Step Seven: Dissociate yourself from the body.

Think about getting lighter and lighter and lighter, until finally your body is relieved of its soul. Apply all of the steps above until you finally are able to completely sever the soul from the body for at least five minutes at a time.

MAGICK AND SPELLS

WHAT IS A SPELL?

First, know this: there are many varieties of magic, and even in those types of magic where spell-work is taught and regarded as effective, there is no general agreement on what magic is, or what it is not, nor what exactly a spell is, nor what it is not.

Most will agree, however, that a spell is merely a manipulation of energy to cause an action or event. Spells are one of many ritual activities that many Wiccans conduct. Not all Wiccans cast spells—spellwork is not a mandatory aspect of Wicca by any means.

Parallels can be drawn between the Wiccan spell and the Christian prayer, for example. Christians sometimes pray to their God in the hopes of changing their lives, or the lives of others. They may pray that a friend does well on a test, or a child recovers from an illness. Some light a prayer candle in their home or church. Such rituals have many similarities to Wiccan spells.

Spells can be designed to attempt to either harm or help others. Thus, there are both evil spells and healing spells. The same magickal processes are used for both.

PHILOSOPHY AND ETHICS

There is little debate about the fact that Wiccans may not cast a spell specifically to harm another. However, there are a lot of gray areas that are the subject of vigorous debate. One example of a gray area is the ethics of a love spell.

Some feel that casting a love spell on a specific target is tantamount to forcing or bending the free will of another. Others feel that such a spell merely makes the spellcaster more attractive to the target, and the target is free to act or not act on whatever impulses he or she might have.

Some feel that it is only acceptable to cast a general love spell; others feel that this too could be construed as forcing the will of others. Some even believe that it's inappropriate to cast a spell to heal a sick friend or family member because a karmic situation may be tampered with. Others feel that it is perfectly altruistic and safe to cast a spell to heal a friend.

Wiccans are prohibited from engaging in spells or other activities which harm others. This is a result of Wiccans' belief in the three-fold law and the Wiccan Rede.

Three-fold Law: "All good that a person does to another returns three-fold in this life; harm is also returned three-fold."

Wiccan Rede: "An it harm none, do what thou wilt."

Before performing a spell, a Wiccan must carefully think through all the possible repercussions of a spell to make certain that it does not have a manipulative, malicious, or overly forceful component. Wiccans believe that spells altar the course of the universe and should, ergo, not be taken lightly.

Not everyone, however, pays as close attention to the Wiccan Rede as they should. Though magickal attacks are uncommon, they do happen. Most agree that it is not acceptable to go on the offensive; a simple defensive spell will be all that is needed.

Basically, there is no one answer to some of these more nuanced areas of spellwork. The important thing is that you be very honest with yourself about your intentions, and decide on your own if a spell violates the Rede. If in doubt, consult with a more experienced Wiccan.

MAGICK & SPELLWORK

Those of you will be practicing alone and not with a coven
will no doubt want to learn some basic spellwork and
magick. After your requisite studies of herbs and pagan
tradition, you may start on the basics. Before proceeding,
make sure you understand how to take a ritual bath, cast a
circle, cleanse wands and other tools, and meditate.
Although it is tempting to skip the basics and dive right in,
your spellwork and your focus will suffer if you are
unprepared!

First, know this: there are many varieties of magic, and
even in those types of magic where spell-work is taught and
regarded as effective, there is no general agreement on
what magic is, or what it is not, nor what exactly a spell is,
nor what it is not.

Some feel that certain objects—such as crystals, herbs, and
tarot cards, have within them a certain causal link to some
realm of human desire—for instance, luck, love, or money.
In natural magic, the object's physical appearance gives it
its particular magical powers and properties. Thus, violet
leaves, which look like hearts, are used in love magic, and
lodestones, which are natural magnetic rocks, are used to
"draw" things (love, money, luck) to the subject of the

spell. Sometimes the place of an object in popular or Wiccan culture lends to its uses—for example, the use of roses in love spells.

An overlapping type of magic includes natural objects but expands to also encompass human-made objects, such as amulets, lucky charms, chalices, wands, tarot cards, and other such things. This form of magic is called Talisman Magic. Objects of magic can be made by the Witch him or herself but are often crafted by an artisan. If an object is commercially purchased, it must be empowered, cleansed, and charged for use. Once the object has been prepared and charged with the energy of the Witch, it is said to be magical in and of itself.

A third popular form of magic is called will-based magic. Those who believe strictly in will based magic have little need for wands or other such props. They believe that visualizing an outcome will bring the reward. This can be likened to many popular theories of life management, such as The Power of Positive Thinking and The Secret.

Regardless of whichever type of magic you find the most compelling, it is important to remember the extent to its efficacy. It is a way of working with subtle energies in conjunction with specific action on behalf of the practitioner. For example, if you wish to do well on a test, it is not enough to merely cast a spell. You must prepare for the test and show up to take it in addition to the casting of the spell or the wearing of a lucky object.

It is important to remember too that magic is not infallible. For example, magic can certainly protect you. But if you go out driving drunk with no seatbelt, there is a limit to its effectiveness. In other words, there is no such thing as a free lunch. Writing even the most effective spell will be for naught if not accompanied with the appropriate common-sense precautions and actions on your part.

CANDLE SPELL

One of the simplest of magical arts which comes under the heading of natural magic is candle burning. The materials are easy to obtain and use an object with which we are all familiar—a candle.

The size and shape of the candles you use is unimportant, although decorative, extra large, ornate, scented, or unusually shaped candles will not be suitable as these may create distractions. The simple slender candles sold for use in the home is perfectly fine, if not ideal. Those who are feeling particularly industrious can make his or her own. Candle kits can be found at specialty and craft stores, and are easy to use.

The candles you use for any type of magical use should be completely unused, and no one but yourself should touch it. Under no circumstances use a candle which has already been lit, even for the most benign purpose. Vibrations picked up by secondhand materials or equipment may disturb and pollute your work.

Once you have purchased or made your ritual candle it has to be 'dressed' before burning so as to establish a psychic link between it and you. By touching the candle during the dressing procedure, you are charging it with our own personal energy and also concentrating the desire of your magical act into the wax. The candle, in this sense, almost becomes like a wand, and is an extension of you. Make sure you dress the candle before it is lit.

To dress it, point the candle to the north. Use a compass to make sure that you are pointing it in the right direction. Rub oil into the candle beginning at the top or North end and work downwards to the half-way point. Always brush in the same direction downwards. This process is then repeated by beginning at the bottom or south end and working up to the middle. The oil that you use is important. This will be discussed later in detail.

The candles you use can be colored in accordance with the following magickal uses:

White- peace and innocence.

Red- strength, courage, sexual potency.

Pink- love and romance.

Yellow- memory

Green- fertility and luck

Blue-protection from evil

Purple- luck in finances

Orange—career matters

For instance, if you wanted to use candle magic to enrich your sex life, you would select a red candle to burn. To pass an exam, burn a yellow candle.

The simplest form of candle magic is to write down your goal on a clean, unused piece of paper. Use paper in a color that matches the candle. As you write your goal, visualize your dream coming true. Visualize your boss giving you a raise, or your business selling out of its product because it has become a wild success.

After you have written down your goal and meditated on it, carefully fold the paper four times. Place the end of the folded paper in the candle flame and set light to it. As it burns, focus on your goal.

Allow the candle to burn till it goes out. Take normal fire safety precautions and keep watch over it as it burns.

If you are conducting a magical ritual which involves another person, such as sending healing powers to a sick person, the second person can be symbolically present during the ritual by another candle.

SAMPLE SPELLS

SPELL TO MEND A WOUNDED HEART

To Ease a Broken Heart you will need the following ingredients (be sure to charge them all before you begin):

Strawberry tea (at least one teabag's worth)
Small wand or stick from a willow tree
Three drops of lavender oil.
pink candles (2)
a mirror
one pink drawstring bag
one quartz crystal
one bowl of china, crystal, or silver
one silver spoon
1 teaspoon dried jasmine
1 tsp. strawberry leaves
1 teaspoon cloves
20 drops strawberry oil

Arrange the materials on a small table. Light an unused, pink candle that has been rubbed in a drop of strawberry oil. Make sure that no one has touched the candle besides you, and make sure that the candle has never been used. Make strawberry tea and when the water is done boiling, let the tea steep. While it steeps, draw a bath and add the lavender. Do not use any light other than the pink candle's light to draw and take the bath.

When you rise from the bath, sip the strawberry tea. Put a dab of strawberry oil on your throat, wrists, and heart. Use the willow wand to cast two circles in a clockwise direction around the table that the materials rest on.

Rub two drops of strawberry oil on the second candle. Make sure that the wick end is pointed north as you do so. Light the second pink candle. Mix all remaining and oils and herbs—except for the strawberry tea leaves from the tea--in the bowl.

While you stir the mixture slowly clockwise with a silver spoon, look at yourself in the mirror and say aloud: "I see the Threefold Goddess within me. Then put the mixture in the pink bag with the crystal. You will carry it with you always. Every time you are tempted to dwell on that which wounded your heart, smell the bag full of herbs. Remind yourself that you are the Threefold Goddess, and you bask in the light of Diana.

When your heart is healed, bury the bag.

HOME PROTECTION SPELL

You will need:

Small mirror
Seven white candles
Bundle of dried sage
Matches
Essential oil of your choosing.
Representation of the Goddess of your choosing.
Representation of the God of your choosing.

As always, the first step is to consecrate the space you will be using, take a ritual bath, and put on your ritual wear.

Place your God and Goddesses representations in the middle of the altar. The next step will be to dress your candles. Kneel before the altar. Using essential oil from an herb or tree with protective qualities, mentally visualize a wall of energy surrounding your home. Rub the candles with the oil, pointing the wicks North as you do so.

Next, go to your altar. After reaching a state of concentration, place a bundle of sage between the effigies of the Goddess and the God. Ring the sage and effigies with your candles. Turn to your Goddess effigy. Continuing to visualize the field of energy surrounding your home, say:

Lunar light protect me!

Then turn to the God and say:

Solar light protect me!

Repeat as you light each candle.
Now, holding the mirror, invoke the Goddess and say:

> *Great Goddess of the Light*
> *Great Goddess of the Sea*
> *Great Goddess of the Land*
> *Let all darkness flee.*

Standing before the altar, hold the mirror facing the candles so that it reflects their flames. Keeping the mirror toward the candles, move slowly clockwise around your altar seven times, repeating the invocation. Continue concentrating on the wall of energy that surrounds your home. Visualize the candle light burning away the bad energy in your home.

Then, invoke the God and say:

> *Great God of the Light*
> *Great God of the Sea*
> *Great God of the Land*
> *Let all darkness flee.*

As you say this, hold the mirror as you have been but move counter clockwise, repeating the invocations.

Charge your home with the protective light of the Goddess and God. Visualize the light streaming through your home and bathing it in light.

When finished, stand once again before the images. Thank the Goddess and the God in any words you wish. Put out the candles, tie them together with white cord and store them in a safe place.

BASIC PROSPERITY SPELL

This is a basic spell that if used correctly, will bring you money.

You will need:

1 gold candle
6 green candles
9 white candles
Pine oil
sea salt or, if you live near the ocean, sand.

Take your ritual bath, put on your ritual wear, and cast the circle. Then carefully dress all candles with pine oil.

Arrange the candles thusly on the altar:

Gold candle in the center
Green candles in a circle around gold candle
White candles in a circle around green candles.

To begin, sprinkle a circle of salt or sand around the altar. Start to concentrate. Visualize yourself walking down the street and finding money, a bank error in which you are given extra funds or even a mound of coupons to your oft-frequented stores.

Light the middle candle and envision the flame acting as a magnet for money.

Circle the altar three times clockwise, visualizing the luck you want.

Say the following three times:

> *As my heart be full with the Goddess' light*
> *Bring money into my sight.*

After the previous saying, snuff out the flames. Place the candles in a green bag, and put them away. Though they cannot be used for another spell, they can serve decorative purposes at a later date.

That's it!

SELF BLESSING

This can be performed on the eve of a Sabbat, during a particularly challenging time, or in honor of a new moon.

The purpose of the ritual is to bring you into closer contact with the Goddess and the God, to feel their blessings, and to reaffirm the relationship you have with them. It may also be used to banish any negative influences which may have formed around the person, to cleanse oneself after contact with someone who has contagious negative energy, or on another person who requires any of the above. After the ritual, it is ideal that the blessed person spend time in meditation, or in solitude, reflecting on that which has transpired. It is also ideal that the participants be sky-clad, though this is not necessary.

You will need:
Sea salt or sand from a beach or riverbank.
Three red or green grapes.
Spring water
White candle

After taking a ritual bath, cast your circle. Sprinkle the salt on the floor and stand on it. Light your candle and enjoy its warmth. Imagine its light and energy surrounding you and mingling with your own energy. Say:

> *Bless me, mother, for I am a child of the earth, and the eyes of the world.*

Dip the fingers of the right hand into the water and touch to your eyelids, first the left, then the right. Say:

> *Blessed be my eyes, that I may see your works and majesty.*

Touch the water to the tip of the nose. Say:

> *Blessed be my nose, that I may breathe the wind and air.*

Touch the water to the top lip, then the bottom, then the tip of the tongue. Say:

> *Blessed be my tongue that I may speak of you.*

Touch the water to your chest. Say:

> *Blessed be my breast, that I may feel your love in my heart.*

Touch your feet, first the left, then the right. Say:

> *Blessed be my feet that I may walk in your ways.*

Eat the grapes, one after the other, and Say

> *Blessed be your bounty that I may enjoy of your gifts.*

Enjoy the candle for as long as you wish. If desired, set it down and meditate. When you exit the circle, try to spend at least an hour in solitude and reflection.

BASIC LOVE SPELL

For this spell, you will need:

2 pink candles

3 cloves

2 teaspoons of black tea

3 pinches cinnamon

3 pinches nutmeg

3 fresh mint leaves

6 fresh rose petals

6 lemon leaves

3 cups pure spring water

Brown sugar

Honey

Brew this tea on a Friday during a waxing moon. Take your ritual bath as usual, but with pink candles. As you bathe, focus on the work you are about to do.

Cleanse and consecrate a tea kettle and teapot. Cast your circle, and light a pink candle to place on your altar. Boil the spring water, pour into tea pot, and place the tea pot on your altar. Let the herbs steep. As it is brewing,

Recite this verse three times:

> *I MAKE THIS TEA BY THE LIGHT OF THE*
> *MOON TO MAKE [lover's name] ONLY FOR ME*
> *SWOON*

Pour in the honey and the sugar, and then add to your cup.
Drink one sip of the tea and say:

> *GODDESS OF LOVE, I BREWED THIS TEA*
> *THAT [lover's name] MAY DESIRE ME!*

On the following Friday, brew another pot of the tea and
share it with the object of your affections. He or she will
soon begin to fall in love with you.

BASIC SPELL TO ATTRACT LOVE

You Will Need:

1 Pink Candle

Rose Incense

Rosemary leaves

4 Drops Tangerine oil

First, dress your candle in Tangerine oil, and take ritual bath by its light. When you emerge, take the candle with you, sit before your altar and concentrate. Think of the qualities you have to give to another, and the qualities you want him/her to be able to give to you.

As you concentrate, sprinkle the rosemary around the candle. Say:

> *I say to the spirits of the Lady above,*
> *I am ready to meet my one true love".*

Say this as many times as needed, and as you do so, imagine a vivid pink light emanating from your body and filling the room. When you are finished, extinguish the flame.

CROSSING PATHS SPELL

You Will Need:

Yellow candles
Yellow thread
Picture of yourself
Picture of intended
Magnet or moonstone
Scissors
Yellow thread
Yling Ylang oil

On a night during the Waxing Moon, gather the above ingredients, dress your candles with the yling ylang oil, and take your ritual bath by their light.

When you emerge, bring the candles. Hold your picture in your left hand, and hold the other picture in your right.

Say:

> *I hold your picture in my hand*
> *By the will of the Lady*
> *You will soon before me stand.*

As you say this, cut the images out of the photos, and then sew them together with the needle and thread. Place the picture underneath the moonstone or magnet on your altar, between two of the yellow candles.

Say:

> *This picture of me,*
> *This picture of you*
> *Now are one when*
> *Once they were two.*

Meditate as long as you need. Though the spell has been cast, you must still continue to send energy to the person you want to see, as well as contact him or her.

PHOENIX LOVE SPELL

You will need:

Four small white stones
Rose petals
Orange seeds
Pink Candle
Rose oil

Dress your candle in rose oil and take the ritual bath by its light. When you emerge, bring your candle with you, and cast your circle.

In the circle, put the white stones down on the points of the compass: one to the north, one to the south, one to the east, and one to the west. In the middle of the circle, scatter a handful of rose petals and orange seeds.

Say:

>*Oranges and roses*
>*Candles and stones*
>*Send me true love*
>*My true love alone*
>*Feather of the Phoenix*

Bring him/her to my sight
Make him/her rise to my vision
The one who is right.

As you say this, concentrate on the one you love, or the type of person you'd like to love.

FIDELITY SPELL

This very simple, very easy spell acts to strengthen the bonds that keep lovers faithful.

You Will Need:

1 lime
Hair From Your Head
Hair From Your Partners Head
Pink candle
Ritual bowl

This spell should ideally be done on a Friday when the moon is waxing. Take your bath by the light of the pink candle. When you emerge, go to your altar. Place the hairs in the ritual bowl and squeeze the lime juice on them, saying:

I am bound to you
You are bound to me
By the light of the moon
So mote it be.

Repeat this as many times as necessary.

CINNAMON SPELL

This spell will add spice to your love life.

You Will Need:

3 Tablespoons Of Cinnamon Powder
A red piece of fabric
A length of red lace
Red candle
Yling Ylang oil
Rose quartz

The Spell:

Dress your candle in the oil and take your ritual bath by its light. When you emerge, cast your circle, and place the cinnamon powder and rose quartz in the fabric. Holding the fabric in your right hand, say,

"Spicing up my love life,

the Goddess in my heart,

Bring me the frenzy this spell will start,

Carry the handkerchief in your bag for at least a week.

ADVANCED WORKS OF MAGICK

WRITING YOUR OWN SPELLS

At some point you will wish to write your own spells. The most important component aspect of spell writing is preparation. Even if following a traditional spell, it should be tailored to your specific needs to be most effective for you. Ergo, it is necessary to know the basics of herbalism, color energy, and astrology.

The very first step is to decide precisely what your desired end result is to be. Before you can start, you must decide where you are going. Be very clear about the outcome you want—visualize it happening and concentrate on it before beginning to create your spell.

When you finally finish writing your spell, make sure that you cast it at an ideal time. You should take into consideration all astrological implications, energy currents, Sabbats, and Moon phases. The Sun and the Moon need to be taken into account. They will no doubt be in different parts of the sky, and this will require some attention. Any basic astrology book should be able to tell you where the sun and moon are at any given time.

Magickal workings for binding or material gain should be initiated when the Moon is Waxing (from New to Full). Spells to send things away or repel bad energy are best performed when the moon is Waning. Of course, there will be the odd emergency and you may find yourself needing a love spell when the moon is Waxing. This is not a catastrophe; but if it is possible to plan ahead, do so.

The highest energy occurs at the Full Moon and, therefore, this is the most powerful time for magickal workings. The New Moon is the next most powerful time for Magick.

As always, remember to schedule your workings for a time of uninterrupted privacy. It is important that you have no distractions. Ideally, it is best to work as late at night as possible. Between midnight and three am is the best time but other times will suffice if this is not possible.

In choosing a place to do your magickal working, choose to cast the circle in a place that is private, quiet and safe. If at all possible, set aside a special place for this purpose only. An spare room, a special corner of your bedroom, the attic, or the yard will do. It is not necessary for the place to be outdoors.

Prior to the night of your magickal working, gather together the things that you will need. Consider the purpose of your ritual and choose your tools accordingly. Select the candle and prepare it, cleanse your wand, and make sure you have an adequate supply of whichever herbs, teas, or tinctures you will need. Make sure that your special area will be free and available.

Prior to your ritual, take a ritual bath and put on ritual jewelry or robes. Some believe in remaining chaste for the 24 hour period before a spell; others in fasting. Whatever makes you feel cleansed, charged with energy, and pure is up to you.

Once your purification process has been completed, you are now ready to begin. Proceed to the special place you have previously chosen in which to perform your magick. You may, if you wish, select music to set the mood. Whatever best fits with your objective, Western or Eastern, modern or old, is fine.

As you use your oils, light your candle or incense (or utilize any other tool you have chosen), you should begin to further intensify the energy that surrounds you. Visualize streams of light coming from your body. Imagine your energy field swelling. Inhale and exhale and visualize energy feeding your lungs and being expelled.

Do not scatter your energy by attempting to do more than one spell at a time.

Remember that Magick can also be expressed as a manipulation of energy. A thought is a form of energy and a visualization is an even more potent manifestation of energy. Visualize the objective you wish to achieve and focus on it. Replay the event over and over in your mind while performing your spell..

The most important consideration when choosing your objective is the Universal Law of Retribution. It is the nature of things that as you send something out it gains momentum, so that, by the time it comes back to you, it is three times stronger. If you do something nice for someone, someone will do something nicer for you.

Your magickal working can last for ten minutes, or all night. You can use tools or you can merely use your hands and your mind. There are no hard and fast rules, but it is advisable to cast your circle, take a ritual bath, and wear ritual attire. Other than that, the mechanics of a spell are entirely up to you.

DIVINATION

TAROT

Although tarot cards were used for fortune-telling in Italy in the 18th century, they were not widely known as divination tools until a French occultist named Alliette designed the first esoteric Tarot deck, adding astrological symbolism and "Egyptian" motifs, and inscribing divinatory text on the cards. These decks, called Ettiella decks, are still available. Later, Mademoiselle Marie-Anne Le Normand, friend and confidante to the wife of Napoleon, later popularized them further.

Englishman Eliphas Lévi passed the idea of Tarot for divination to the English-speaking world, and wrote a book called Transcendental Magic that related Tarot cards to Kabbalah and the four elements of Alchemy, and described them as a method for divination.

Tarot became increasingly popular beginning in 1910, with the publication of the Rider-Waite-Smith Tarot deck. This is till one of the most used and most common decks today. These cards have renderings symbolizing divinatory meanings on them, making them more pleasing to the eye.

Tarot reading uses the cards as a way to gain insight into the current and future paths of the subject. Some believe they are guided by a spiritual force, such as Gaia. Others believe that the cards help them link to a collective consciousness, and ambient energy waves.

The deck is comprised of two broad categories: the major and minor arcane. The minor arcana cards are divided into four suites: swords, cups, pentacles, and wands. The major arcana cards may signify different people or attributes, with each card's essence giving insight about the subject's emotional and physical characteristics. For instance, "Joy" is a card in the major arcana, as is "Strength", and "Death".

There are many books that thoroughly discuss the role of the tarot in the art of divination. Some regard the four suits as associated with the four elements: Swords with air, Wands with fire, Cups with water and Pentacles with earth. There are many takes on the tarot, some feeling that the tarot correspond with astrology, others linking it to Pythagorean numerology, and still others connecting Tarot with the Kabbalah, or the I Ching.

To perform a Tarot reading, the Tarot deck is typically shuffled and cards are laid out in a specific pattern, called a "spread". The cards are then interpreted by the reader.

The cards might shed light on the subject's thoughts and desires, or on past, present, and future events.

Some common spreads include the Celtic Cross, wherein five cards are arranged in a cross and four placed vertically to the right of the cross. Another card is placed horizontally across the central card of the cross. The central card of the cross is frequently the card that indicates the characteristics of the querent, or subject. It is referred to as the "significator". The crossing card often represents an obstacle they must face. The rest of the cards may indicate where the person is on his or her journey to a certain outcome.

In the three-card spread, which is an excellent beginner spread, three cards are used, with the first representing the past, the second the present, the third the future.

Tarot is a magnificently elegant art form. There is far more to it than can be included in the scope of this book. But with all magical objects, it is important to find a deck that speaks to you, and that you connect with. I personally prefer the Hanson-Roberts tarot deck to the Rider-Waite, though the Rider-Waite is by far more popular. There is no "right" or "wrong" deck; merely pick the one that speaks to you.

NUMEROLOGY

Numerology is any of many systems that look for aspects of the divine or the pre-ordained in the relationship between numbers and physical objects or living beings.

Many mathematicians agree with Wiccans that nature in general corresponds to numeric patterns. Wiccans, however, take this a step further. Many believe that any and every aspect of our lives, and the lives of everything around us follows a numeric pattern which can be used to establish compatibility, physical destiny, or Karmic destiny. Numerology Readings are often used as a companion to an Astrological Reading.

One such method of using numbers for the purposes of divination is to reduce a word by digit summing, then reach a conclusion based on the single digit that results.

This involves taking the sum of all of the digits in a number, and repeating the process until a single-digit is produced. For a word, the values corresponding to each letter's place in the alphabet (e.g., A=1, B=2, through Z=26)

Examples:

KRISTINA
$= 16 + 18 + 9 + 19 + 20 + 9 + 14 + 1$
$= 88$
$= 16$
$= 7$

Depending on the system of numerology to which you adhere, the number 7 will have certain significance.

Different methods of calculation exist, including Chaldean, Pythagorean, Hebraic, Phonetic, Japanese, Arabic, and Indian.

In most of these systems, a number is assigned certain characteristics, values, and a male or female essence. Analysis of these numbers provides insights into many different aspects of the life of the subject or querent. Defining and describing these systems are beyond the scope of this book; a thorough numeric reading can be fifty pages or longer! But, this overview should give you enough information to allow you to decide if numerology is a method of divination that interests you.

PALMSTRY

Palmistry is the art of divination through the study of the palm. The practice is found all over the world, with numerous cultural variations. Those who practice this art form are generally called palmists, palm readers, handanalysts , hand readers, or chirologists.

Palmistry can trace its roots back to Indian (Hindu) Astrology (known in Sanskrit as Jyotish) and Roma (gypsy) fortune tellers. Modern palmists, however, often combine traditional predictive techniques with psychology, holistic healing, and alternative methods of divination.

The basic idea of palmistry is that one can evaluate person's character or destiny by "reading" the palm of that person's hand. Various lines in the palm, as well as palm shape and finger length, are interpreted by their relative sizes, depth, qualities, and intersections. Some readers will also give weight to the quality and texture of the fingernails, fingerprints, skin color, and hand flexibility.

Methods and systems vary by practitioner and tradition, but the basic idea is that each area of the palm and fingers is related to a god or goddess. The physical characteristics and appearance of that area serves to give insight as to the nature of the corresponding attribute of the subject. For example, the ring finger is associated with the Greek god Apollo. The physical characteristics of the ring finger indicate the subject's relationship to art, music, aesthetics, fame, and harmony.

Hand shapes can also be of significance. They are often divided into four or five major types, indicating character traits corresponding to the four elements.

For example, Earth hands have wide palms, strong muscles, coarse skin, and a flushed color. Air hands have square or rectangular palms with long fingers and dry skin. Water hands have a long palm with long fingers. Fire hands have a square or rectangle shaped palm, flushed, and shorter fingers.

The lines, of course, are very important as well. Each line, no matter how small, can deliver insight into the temperament and destiny of the subject. However, the heart line, the head line, and the life line can be considered the most important.

The heart line is towards the top of the palm, under the fingers. Usually line is read as starting from the edge of the palm under the little finger or ring finger, and continuing across the palm towards the thumb. This line represents matters of the heart, and indicates emotional stability, romantic possibilities, and cardiac health.

The head line starts at the edge of the palm under the index finger and goes to the outside edge of the palm. This line represents learning style, intellectual capacity, communication style, etc.

The life line extends from the edge of the palm above the thumb and goes in an arch towards the wrist. This line is believed to represent the subject's physical health and general well being. It can also serve to predict or indicate major life changes, but does not necessarily indicate the length of a person's life.

Many, many other characteristics of the hands and fingers have significance in palmistry. Again, describing all of them can fill a whole new book! But this should be enough to give you an idea as to what exactly a palmist is and does.

LEAF READING

Leaf reading is an elegant, ancient form of divination. The skill of reading tea leaves is called Tasseography. Like all other forms of divination, however, there are variations in methodology and philosophy. I will give you the basic idea of what, exactly it means to read someone's tea leaves. Keep in mind, again, that this subject alone could fill a whole other book, and this is just the basics.

First, let your subject choose a type of tea. The tea should have whole leaves that are loose, and shouldn't be too powdery.

Then, boil water, and as the water starts to boil, have the subject add the leaves to the water. Once the kettle whistles and you know the tea is ready, pour it into a wide, large, white cup. It must be white, or a very light color to allow you to see the leaves and the patterns they form.

Let the tea cool slightly. Have the subject meditate on what specific question, if any, he or she has. When the tea is almost at room temperature, have your subject sip it and concentrate on the question at hand.

Instruct your subject to leave a tiny bit of liquid and most of the tea leaves in the bottom of the cup. When the subject finishes, take the cup in your left hand and swirl it around clockwise three times. As you do so, cover the top of the cup with your right hand, making sure to swirl the leaves completely up and around the sides and rim of the cup.

After you have done so, the leaves should now be clumped together in several different places on the cups inside.

These groups of leaves form the symbols that you will read. You should always begin the interpretation by looking for the simplest symbols first. Several of the leaf clumps may clearly form shapes, letters or numbers.

Triangles = good karma

Squares = the need for caution

Circles = great success

Letters refer to the names of loved ones.

Numbers indicate spaces of time.

Most of the clumps, however, will form shapes.

Acorn: financial success

Angel: good news

Kangaroo: harmony at home

Kettle: a sign of peace and tranquility in the home

Ladder: material prosperity

Lock: obstacles or conflicts

Arrow: bad news in love

Axe: possible danger

Candle: a positive future outcome to a present situation.

Pig: greed

Cat: deceit

Snake: an enemy nearby

The symbols go on and on. Most have fairly obvious meanings. But there are plenty of sources to allow you to find and assign meaning to even the most esoteric of symbols.

The symbols will generally form a pattern in the cup. This also has significance.

Examine the cup clockwise to predict events as they unfold in the future.

The handle of the teacup represents the time and place of the reading.

Hold the cup in your left hand, as if you were going to sip from it, and envision a line across the bottom of the cup from the handle to the opposite side. This opposing side will indicate six months into the future.

The top of the cup indicates three months into the future and the part furthest to the bottom indicates nine months ahead. The cup, as you can see, is divided much like the numbers on the clock.

If all of the symbols fall in a clear clockwise spiral within the cup, the top of the spiral is when an event will take place, and the others are the resulting actions or changes.

Symbols on the rim represent important changes or events. Symbols on the sides of the cup represent events of lesser significance. Symbols on the bottom indicate situations that are in flux, and subject to change abruptly.

Tea leaf reading, as you can see, is an elegant and complicated art form. Centuries of tradition and study have gone into its development. If mastered, however, it can yield excellent results.

SCRYING

Scrying (also called crystal gazing) practice that involves seeing things supernaturally in a medium for purposes of divination. The media used are magickal objects that are reflective, translucent, or luminescent. Thus, commonly used items for divination include crystal balls, crystals, water, fire, and mirrors. The visions seen in the objects are thought to come from the Goddess or God, spirits, the pychic mind, or the collective unconscious.

One common version of scrying, popularized as urban legend or folkore, held that young women, gazing into a mirror in a darkened room could see their future husband's face in the mirror — or a skull if their fate was to die before they married.

One method of scrying involves a crystal ball, wherein the seer works herself or himself into a trance. Initially, the medium serves as a focus for the meditation. The scryer begins a then begins free association, looking into the ball to look for and identify the images that appear within. This deepens the trance and ends in the final stage in which details and defined images seem to be projected within the medium itself, or directly within the mind's eye of the scryer. This allows the scryer to "see" the future, or the present in another location.

Few, in my experience, have the psychic depths or openness to become a scryer. It takes practice, and an ability to tap into ambient energies. Those who can scry, however, are rarely mistaken their predictions.

PENDULUM

Pendulums can be used in divination. A pendulum can be a crystal, coin, pendant, or medal on a string. In one approach the user first determines which direction (left-right, up-down) will indicate "yes" and which "no." The user will then proceed to ask the pendulum specific questions, and wait to see into which direction the pendulum settles.

In another form of divination, the pendulum is used with a piece of paper or cloth that has "yes" and "no" written on it. The person holding the pendulum aims to hold it as still and steady as possible over the center of the paper. An interviewer may then ask questions to the person holding the pendulum, and it swings by minute in the direction of the answer.

RUNE MAGICK

The earliest runic inscriptions date from ca. 150. The three best known runic alphabets are:

* the Elder Futhark (ca. 150–800)
* the Anglo-Saxon Futhorc (400–1100)
* the Younger Futhark (800–1100)

These all can further be divided, but the categories and significances go beyond the scope of the section of this book.

The runes were either invented by or presented to the Germanic peoples in the 1st or 2nd century, and in old Scandinavian belief systems, the runes were of divine origin. Their originator was held to be the god Odin, and it was said that he received the runes after several nights of sacrifice in which he hung wounded, thirsty, and hungry from a tree.

Runic divination is a modern practice of divination based on interpretation of the Runic Systems. Runic divination as it is now practiced has strayed from its original historical framework. Some modern authors like Stephen Flowers have based their systems on Hermeticism and classical Occultism, while others have been inspired by modern metaphysical and New Age techniques. Runes can be made of clay, stone tiles, crystals, or polished stones. There is also a school of thought that attempts to link Runic Divination with Tarot.

Rune work is complicated and takes patience and practice. The definitive sources on Runic Divination are:

Futhark: A Handbook of Rune Magic (1984),

Runelore: A Handbook of Esoteric Runology (1987)

At The Well of Wyrd (1988)

ASTROLOGY

Astrology, in the most general sense, is a group of beliefs in which knowledge of the relative positions of celestial bodies can aid in divination and analysis.

Practitioners of astrology are referred to as Astrologists, and interpret the positions of certain celestial bodies' influence on the world and her human inhabitants.

Though the position of celestial body can be considered and evaluated in an Astrological reading, the Sun, Moon, the planets, and the stars are generally of the most importance. The frame of reference for determining their positions are the tropical or sidereal zodiacal signs, the horizon, and midheaven on the other. This latter frame is typically further divided into the twelve astrological houses, which correspond to the twelve signs of the zodiac. Over the centuries, however, the twelve zodiacal signs in

Western astrology have shifted to the point of no longer corresponding to the same part of the sky as their original constellations.

The zodiac is the belt or band of constellations through which the Sun, Moon, and planets move. Twelve cycles of the Moon — the months — coincide with one solar year, and as such, the designation of twelve zodiacal signs corresponding with twelve different constellations was a logical conclusion.

One's zodiacal sign is calculated to correspond to the moment of an individual's birth. The position of the sun in the sky gives the individual his or her sun sign; the position of the moon gives him or her a moon sign. Commonly, in the West, much attention has been given to the Sun signs. For example, in the horoscope section of a magazine, the signs listed are all sun signs. The moon sign, however, is just as important.

A complete horoscope goes far beyond merely the sun and the moon, however. A complete horoscope is a chart divided into twelve different celestial houses. On this chart appears the location of the various positions of heavenly bodies on a given date and time based on astronomical tables.

A horoscope charting the positions of the celestial bodies on the birthday of a subject will tell of the subject's personality, strengths, weaknesses, and future challenges. A horoscope of a particular day can have different meanings for people according to their respective astrological signs.

Astrology is far more complicated and elegant than most people realize. It goes above and beyond the mere act of flipping to the back of Glamour or Cosmo and reading a paragraph. Real astrology involves an intimate knowledge of astronomy, some physics, and a talent for divination. There are volumes of books on the market that can teach exactly how to make a chart, and how to interpret it for yourself or for another.

But basically, figuring out the position of one's moon, sun, and rising is enough for the beginner to start to notice the effect of the cosmos on his or her path and circumstance.

HERBALISM

BASIC MAGICKAL HERBALISM

What follows is a concise list of herbs and their magickal
properties.

The *Back to Eden* book is also excellent for those who are
interested in homeopathic and natural medicine. Though
by no means exhaustive, this list should be enough to get
you started in figuring out what sort of herb garden to
plant, and later, this will also be enough to help you
understand the design of other people's spells. Using other
people's spells is perfectly acceptable, but when you
become very advanced, you will want to create your own
spells and charms. This will be impossible to do without a
basic understanding of herbs.

Use caution when ingesting any herbs. Just because the
herbs are of the earth, and not synthetic, doesn't mean they
won't affect you. I can assure you that they will. White
willow bark, for instance, has been used in painkillers.
Valerian root can have a valium-like effect. Peppermint can
settle the stomach. A catnip potion will make you sleepy. A
mugwort potion will stimulate menstrual flow and calm
nerves. A St. John's Wort potion for protection will lift your
mood. You should be aware of the medicinal properties of
every herb you ingest and also, remember more is not

necessarily better. Herbs are to be used with as much care as synthetic medication.

USES OF HERBS AND SAMPLE POTIONS

Most likely you've heard the word "potion" in movies and TV shows. Witches do indeed brew potions. Potions are simply teas prepared during a selected lunar phase, and often used in conjunction with a ritual or spell.

An infusion is a strong tea, often made with fruit instead of leaves. Lemon, orange peel and apples can be made into infusions. To make them, simply soak the ingredients in water that you have brought to a boil. After you pour the hot water over the ingredients, cover the cup, and let it steep. You may drink the infusion, or even bathe with it.

Solar infusions are much like the infusions described above, except the tea is not boiled. The ingredients are added to the water and placed in the sun until the tea becomes warm. It's good to work with the astrological signs here if possible, but good results can come even if you don't take astrology into account. Another twist on the infusion is to make a lunar infusion, in which the tea sits out under the moon. Choose the best moon signs and phases here.

A decoction is like an infusion, but instead of dried fruit, it uses roots or other herbs with properties that are not easily extracted. Roots, seeds, and stems make good decoctions. Begin with cold water, and add the toughest roots first. Bring to a boil and simmer for about 30 minutes covered. Then let the mixture cool completely. If adding leaves or dried herbs to a decoction, you can take the decoction off the stove and steep your less hardy ingredients as you would an infusion. Be sure to cover throughout the process so the essence of the ingredients don't float away in the steam. When it's done, strain, and use the result.

Tinctures are another type of concoction you can make from herbs and plants. These are very good for homeopathic medicine, and I recommend consulting the book *Back to Eden* for a suggested list of useful plants. Tinctures are also good if you want to be able to store what you make, as tinctures contain alcohol. To make one, get a mason jar with a tight lid, and fill it with 4 oz. of herb and 8 oz. of alcohol—edible alcohol such as brandy or vodka, of course, if you plan on ingesting it. Seal the jar and keep it out of sunlight, at room temperature, for two weeks. For best results, initiate this process on the new moon and finish on the full moon. Be sure to swish the herbs around in the jar daily. When you finally open it, strain the mixture and store the result in an amber or blue colored bottle so it will not be degraded by sunlight.

A wash is a weak tea or infusion that is used externally, for bathing, for anointing, or for homeopathic practices.

A mild wash of 1/4oz. herb to one pint boiling water -- can be used to clean magickal tools, crystals, or talismans. You can even put it in a spray bottle if you'd like to spray the wash on, say, your altar, or other objects in your home. If you don't want to use a spray bottle, however, dip a leafy tree branch in the wash and shake the droplets out.

To make an ointment or balm, simply melt vegetable shortening or Crisco into a liquid form over medium heat. Add your herbs (one part herbs to three parts Crisco or lard or whatever) cover, and let simmer for about ten minutes. Strain out the herbs and store the remaining liquid in an airtight jar. This is for external use, and are not only perfect for Magick, but can be packaged prettily and sold or given as gifts.

Perfumes are made by blending essential oils together to create a fragrance. Choose essential oils and then add them to 1/4 cup rubbing alcohol, 1/4 cup witch hazel tincture, and 1/2 cup water. Shake it up, and you have perfume. As you get more experienced, you'll learn how to blend the oils so that the "notes" come out properly. Vanilla, for instance, makes a good top note and patchouli can make an excellent base. One of my favorite fragrances is a mix of amber, vanilla, and patchouli.

Oils can, of course, be expensive, but with a little practice, you can make them at home. Crush your herbs or flower petals and put them in a jar. Pour warmed safflower, olive, grapeseed, or almond oil on the herbs and steep for 48 hours in sunlight. Strain and repeat, adding fresh herbs. Do this as many times as necessary—some lightly scented flowers will require a lot of repetitions, so be patient. Store the result in dark bottles, away from sunlight.

For those who have little patience, time, or confidence to make their own oils and tinctures, flower essences are very powerful and can be made with little time or energy. These simple potions work on energetic and psychic levels. Pick a flower and place the petals in fresh spring water along with gems, crystals, and whatever other energies you'd like to add. Set the water in full sunlight for several hours. You can add brandy as a preservative. Again, these are great for ceremony, but also can be given as gifts or sold at farmer's markets.

Gem elixirs are made like flower essences, but by using crystals, rocks, and gems instead of flowers.

These are a few suggestions for making magickal potions to get you started, so you can peruse the list of herbs with purpose. You can make adjustments to the recipes all you like because the most important part of these potions is your Magickal energy. Enchant your herbs and charge your potions at the appropriate moon phases if it is not possible to create them at the ideal time.

LIST OF HERBS:

Ague Weed: a protection herb. Also called "Boneset".

Agrimony: acts as a deflective shield; sends back bad energy.

Angelica: highly protective. Can be used as an amulet.

Anise: Good for bringing about changes in attitude, encouraging positive thinking.

Apple/Apple blossoms for love, peace, and contentment.

Ash Cleansing and purification

Asafetida: a very strong protective herb. Can be used to purify spaces that have been contaminated with bad energy.

Alfalfa: for financial success.

Allspice: works with other herbs to bring general good luck. Best as a booster with other herbs.

Althea: attracts good energy and good spirits.

Angelica: keeps away evil energy and evil spirits; can be used as an amulet.

Bergamot: sharpens the intuition.

Bistort: encourages material wealth.

Balm of Gilead: grounding and protective.

Barberry: used for hexing and dooming spaces to bitterness. As such, it should be used with great care.

Bayberry: casts a somber pall on the subject of any spell or tincture that uses Bayberry; encourages reflection.

Basil: for social success; encourages gregariousness.

Bay: induces prophetic dreams and visions; good for general luck and attraction of positive energy.

Benzoin: great to use as a booster, it magnifies the properties of other herbs.

Bergamot: protection and prosperity.

Betony: for removing negative energy; can be used to purify a space or object.

Blueberry: protective, particularly of bad energies.

Bindweed: used to dull the negative energies and intentions of others.

Bistort: fertility and sexual potency.

Broom Tops: purification and protection.

Black Snakeroot: an aphrodisiac and somewhat of a "love potion number 9"

Buchu leaves: used for psychic development

Cherry blossoms: bring honesty and encourages reflection.

Chamomile: soothes and calms nervousness and restlessness.

Caraway Seeds: protective; helps sharpen the memory.

Carnation: protection.

Camphor: to cleanse and sterilize.

Cardamom: a powerful love herb.

Clove: brings strength of will and resolve; excellent for blending with other herbs.

Cinnamon: an aphrodisiac. Cinnamon also helps prevent spikes in blood sugar, and can be a natural insecticide. Sprinkle on countertops or tabletops to get rid of ants.

Cedar: protection, purification.

Cherry Blossoms: associated with honesty and truth.

Capsicum (Cayenne): gives strength, resolve, and energy.

Coriander: used for love and friendship.

Citronella: for attraction. Good for attracting friends and business.

Cumin: can control impulses towards infidelity; encourages closeness and openness.

Calendula: induces prophetic dreams.

Dogbane: removes deception and dishonesty.

Deerstongue: acts to filter away bad energy and bad vibes.

Dill: for love and protection.

Devil's Bit: commanding and compelling.

Dragon's Blood: Power and protection.

Elder: highly protective.

Elecampane: for love charms of all kinds.

Eucalyptus: highly protective in areas of health. Also used for purification.

Elm bark: stops slander and general negativity.

Fennel: can remove hexes and create an unexpected turn of events.

Frankincense: associated with the male energies and acts as a sound "white" magical base to receive other herbs or oils.

Five Finger Grass: (cinquefoil) money spells.

Fenugreek: brings luck and success.

Frangipani: an attraction or "magnetic" herb. Use to bring things to you.

Foxglove: exposes lying and deception.

Grains of Paradise: attracts good fortune and good luck.

Ginger: used to induce passion. A good catalyst to add to formulas for romantic love. Also can aid in digestion.

Geranium: used to lift the spirits and banish negativity. Can also be used in fertility potions.

Heliotrope: another sun herb. Attracts wealth and good spirits.

Honey: binds and attracts, seduces, charms.

Honeysuckle: best for rectifying situations of infidelity.

Hawthorn: used for protection, purification and banishing.

Hazel: excellent for protection and to inspire others to trust you.

Hemlock: one of the foremost hexing agents. Added to any oil or incense to reverse its meaning.

Hyacinth: Attracts love, luck and brings peace of mind and restful sleep.

Heather: protects.

Hyssop: anointing, blessing, consecrating, purifying.

Irish moss: used to ensure success and growth in the long term.

Jasmine: essentially a seduction herb and aphrodisiac.

Juniper berries: a power herb which also acts as an aphrodisiac.

Lavender: cleanses, protects, can be used for uncrossing. Soothes and calms nerves, anxiety, and insomnia.

Lemon or Lemon blossoms: can used in love formulas to both repel and attract depending on the recipe.

Licorice: an aphrodisiac. Also aids in digestion.

Lemon Verbena: for luck, strengthening, and attracting.

Lemon Grass: is a good general power herb that can magnify the properties of other herbs when used correctly.

Lilac: brings peace and harmony. Is excellent for reversing a hex; encourages peace and harmony.

Lobelia: to be used with the utmost care as it can be fatal if swallowed. As such, it poisons the effects of other herbs and can reverse them.

Lotus: associated with the magic of the ancients.

Lily of the Valley: used for calming and blessing.

Lime: To keep a lover faithful and to strengthen a relationship that is already in place.

Lovage: an "Attracting" herb. Does not need to be used just for romance; can be used to attract colleagues or friends.

Marjoram: protective - especially in matters of love. Can also protect the home and hearth.

Mint: peppermint is used as a stimulant and can give energy to the lethargic. Spearmint is calming. Both aid in digestion. Both aid in giving clarity and reason.

Mistletoe: for protection and to uncross a hex.

Myrtle: love, fertility, protection and healing.

Masterwort: power, strength and courage with good protective qualities. .

Mimosa: a commanding herb which also inspires deference in others.

Motherwort: a protecting herb.

Mugwort: clairvoyance, and the summoning of spirits.

Mullien: lends courage and helps troubles be laid to rest.

Neroli: (bitter orange) a magnetic oil used for attracting.

Orange or Orange Blossoms:
attracting, drawing, can be used in love
potions.

Orris: a focusing herb, used to focus the
power of other herbs it is combined
with. Also used as a "love herb"

Oakmoss: a power herb.

Patchouli: an herb of power and
manifestation, for materializing one's
wishes. Encourages sensuality and can
act as an aphrodisiac.

Pennyroyal: Cleanses and protects.
Brings harmony and is helpful in times
of domestic unrest.

Peppermint: use to create change and
get things moving.

Pine: excellent for cleansing and uncrossing, protecting or refocusing. Energizing and grounding at the same time.

Poppy Seeds: for dreams, visions, and to induce a peaceful, relaxed states.

Queen of the Meadow: helps create new opportunities

Rose: general, nonspecific love. Can be mixed with other herbs for good results.

Rosemary: binds things (or people) together in a loving, gentle manner. Can also use for purification.

Rose Geranium: Reverses misfortune and can be used with other herbs to bless a new home.

Rue: highly protective. Often used in consecration rituals.

Sassafrass: Commanding and twisting.

Sandalwood: used to heighten spiritual vibrations, to cleanse, heal and protect.

Slippery Elm: a highly focused protection herb, especially against negative energy.

Snakeroot: can help you let go of a person, thing, or burdensome idea.

St. Johns wort: a quick-acting protection herb. Works quickly to reverse negativity.

Sweetpea: an attraction oil used to draw friends or lovers, loyalty and affection.

Solomon's Seal: an uncrossing herb associated with luck and wisdom. Brings hunches, intuition and dreams.

Strawberry: used to draw fortunate circumstances into one's life.

Squill root: very powerful for money

Thyme: encourages positive vibrations and actions.

Tormentil: (blood root) a commanding herb that can be used for good or ill.

Vanilla: a subtle seduction agent. Can also be used as a gentle aphrodisiac. Induces passion.

Vetivert: (khus khus) Excellent for uncrossing, protecting, cleansing and then refocusing.

Violet: for truth. Guards against deception and creates an atmosphere of trust and honesty.

HEALING

AURA READING

An aura is a subtle field of luminous energy surrounding a person or a being, much like a halo. An aura is composed of soul vibrations or chakras, and may reflect the moods, personal characteristics, or thoughts of the person it surrounds. Auras are related to the etheric body but still can reflect the general health of the physical body. They are not light but a translation of the energy of the body that they envelop. They are not visible in complete darkness, and if a part of a person is hidden (say behind a wall or piece of furniture) that portion of the aura will be hidden as well.

It is believed that auras may be viewed by the naked eye, though some may need to go through focused training in order to consistently see auras. Auras are thought of as a web of energy that can act as a shield, having separate layers that are all part of this web.

Once you get in tune with the ability to see auras, you will see swirls of light around individuals, or even plants or animals. In most, the aura is of an even shape and thickness, with a changing and swirling color pattern. It extends anywhere from twelve to eighteen inches from the periphery of the physical form.

With practice and a little know how, one can learn to read an aura by its color, thickness, and strength. If the subject is healthy, physically and mentally, the aura will be strong, glowing, and consistent. If not, spots of irregular color or total blackness may appear. In the following sections, you will learn the basics of aura healing and reading.

AURIC HEALING

Our auras are like magnets for energy. It is important to cleanse our auras to liberate them from bad, negative, or even just plain unwanted energies. There are many ways to do this.

One if the easiest ways to clean your own aura is to use clean your hands with spring water, and then your fingers as a comb, and comb the space surrounding your body from head to toe. While doing so, take deep breaths and visualize your aura as it is cleaned and invigorated.

Another method of aura cleansing involves two people. This process is a simple transfer of energy from a healer to the afflicted. The healer will look over your aura carefully to see if there are any inconsistencies in color, thickness, or clarity. He or she will physically look at you, or will use her hands to scan the area that surrounds you in order to feel for a dead, or overly charged spot. This generally takes a fairly experienced practitioner.

Once the afflicted areas have been identified, the healer and the recipient ground and center themselves. The healer then sends energy drawn from the Earth, or from the spirit, depending on his or her school of thought on the matter.

This energy is sent to the area will crowd and finally push out the negative energies, and the negative will seep down the grounding cord to be recycled and purified by the Earth. The healer will then seal the aura with white energy. This process can take five minutes to an hour depending on the extent of the auric damage.

Another option is Auric Surgery. After grounding and centering, the healer will open up a small vortex of energy, and then "cut" and remove the damaged portion from the recipient's aura, and then places it into the energy vortex. The resulting void in the recipient's aura is then filled with good energy from the healer, and then sealed with white energy. The vortex will then be closed. The healer should then step away from the recipient, shake hands in a downwards motion to shake off any bad residue, and then wash his or her hands.

COLOR MAGICK

Sometimes, the aura will not necessarily be spotty or damaged; it will merely be faded or lacking in a particular color. Once you get in touch with your auric field, you may notice this corresponds with days when you feel tired, out of sorts, or just sort of listless in general.

Below is a list of colors in auras, and how they can be used to heal or read an aura. All colors are useful; there are no colors that are superior to or better than any other color. They merely all have different and necessary properties.

White: Universal, pure energy. Most neutral, and can be accepted and used by all.

Red: Energizer, invigorator clears blockages, warms, reduces joint discomfort.

Orange: Freeing color; heals both physical and mental levels, releases repressions, liberates stuck emotions or impulses

Yellow: Heals the nervous system and invigorates the brain and mental energies.

Green: Universal healing color. It is most useful for bringing harmony, and is an all purpose healer.

Blue: Cleansing, cooling; helps cure sore throats, helps slow bleeding, brings down temperatures, encourages communication, and soothes chronic pain and inflammation

Indigo: Purifies; can help with many mental illnesses or chemical imbalances

Violet: Used almost exclusively for spiritually related disorders, and sometimes in the cases of psychological illness.

Depending on what ails the afflicted, the aura can be expansive and full of the vibrant colors, or it can be very tightly knit to the body, murky, and cloudy.

To clarify, however: the colors appearing within the aura that reflect the general well-being and state of the soul and spiritual self. It is the clarity and quality of the colors.

Before you can start healing people, or charging layers or colors of an aura, it is important to learn how to read an aura, afflicted or not.

RED: those with a particularly red aura, or an aura primarily consisting of red, is usually vigorous, sexual, and energetic. He or she is usually prone to competition and/or aggressiveness.

ORANGE: Orange in the aura signifies creativity regeneration. An abundance of radiant orange indicates a person who could be an excellent healer, or is merely extremely open minded and accepting of others. The positive shades indicate thoughtfulness, and consideration. Muddier shades indicate laziness or repression.

YELLOW: Yellow is the color of the mind and intellect. How it blends with other colors, especially red and orange, indicates how one's intellectual stamina and capacity is used. Where yellow primarily present in the higher parts of the aura, indicates a more inspired mental consciousness. When it is pooled in the lower half of the aura, it indicates more analytical thought. When yellow is murky in color, blended with brown, gray, or black, it indicates a person who uses the power of mind for manipulation or greed.

When blended with a muddy or murky green, it indicates resentment and jealousy.

GREEN: Green is the color of balance and harmony. When green is pooled at the bottom of the aura and appears murky, it indicates a potential for jealousy and possessiveness. A very murky green indicates depression. When collected mostly in the outer layers of the aura it indicates a person who is sympathetic, peaceful, and compassionate.

BLUE: blue is the color of spirit, tranquility, and the heavens. For the most part, although not always, the presence of blue within the aura is a positive statement.

INDIGO: Indigo is blue with a small amount of clear red. It indicates selfless spirituality and pursuit of knowledge. Its absence within the aura is as important as its presence.

VIOLET: violet indicates passion and love. Violet is only present when the individual has made a commitment to some spiritual path and is guided by higher consciousness in its pursuit.

BROWN: Its presence reflects some negative condition, depending on the color with which it is mixed

BLACK: black is the absence of all color and indicates either a spiritual sickness, or the presence of evil. It is for you to decide if the person is merely suffering from a spiritual illness and requires healing, or is so malicious as to have a corroded aura.

WHITE: White is perfect balance and harmony. White never originates and emanates from within the human aura; it is always received.

While the color is important, more important is its quality. Soft, pastel shades generally indicate a positive condition, while dark, murky, and muddy shades tend to indicate a more negative condition.

BASIC CRYSTAL SELECTION AND CARE

Crystals can be chosen to aid in specific spells, and for meditative practices. When it comes to selecting the crystals you will work with, I would recommend that you go to a store that will allow you to not only look at, but touch them. You will find that the right crystal will identify itself quickly. Though there are many reputable online stores that sell crystals, it is difficult to asses their individual energies and vibrations without touching and holding them.

While perusing gems and crystals you may find that a particular item draws you to it. Follow your instincts. Your body and psyche needs all 7 colors: red, orange, yellow, green, blue, indigo and violet and you may unconsciously be drawn to the gems or crystals that are most appropriate for you.

CHARGING & CLEASING OF CRYSTALS

Before you start to use your crystals you should clean and charge them to remove any negative energy or vibrations from others who may have handled them. There are several easy ways to cleanse your crystals:

Bathing

Soak your crystal in one cup of sea salt dissolved in one quart of purified or spring water. Use a glass or porcelain bowl as silver or copper may interfere with the crystals' natural vibrations. When you place them in the bowl, meditate on them and ask that they are cleared. Leave them for at least an hour but they can soak for a day without harm.

Sunshine Bath

Place your crystal in direct sunlight for at least four hours. When you place each crystal, meditate and ask that the crystal is cleared.

Moonlight Bath

Place your crystal in the light of a full moon for at least four ours. When you place each crystal, meditate and ask that the crystal is cleared.

Burying

Wrap your crystal in cotton, silk or linen and bury it in a place you feel comfortable for at least 24 hours.

After you have used one or more of these methods, they are ready to be charged. You will learn about charging Magickal objects in the section about your wand. The lesson in that section can be applied to any talisman or Magickal object. After cleansing and charging you should never let anyone touch your crystals. Should this accidentally happen, clean and charge them again before using them in your work.

PROPERTIES OF CRYSTALS, STONES, AND GEMS

AVENTURINE: A good luck stone, especially in financial matters. Stimulates creativity, intelligence and perception. A great healing stone, it clears negative energy and vibrations as well as restoring general well being.

AGATE: General protection and healing, increases courage, self-confidence, and energy and promotes longevity. Solid, grounding.

AMETHYST: Reduces negative emotions (anger, impatience, nightmares); improves psychic abilities and imagery.

BLOODSTONE: An intense healing stone. It revitalizes love, relationships and friendships. It brings purification, orderliness, prosperity, and instills wisdom, enhances creativity, and supports decision making. Warrior stone for overcoming obstacles, calm ones fears of a real or perceived enemy, Boosts strength and courage and attracts wealth, healing, charity.

CITRINE: Reduces anxiety, fear, and depression; improves problem-solving, memory, willpower, and clarity.

CLEAR QUARTZ: Inner strength, amplifies the properties of other gemstones, strength. Probably the most versatile multi-purpose healing stone. Easy to cleanse, store info/energy in, program or amplify energy and healing with. Can both draw and send energy. Powerful clear ones for meditation, sending & receiving guidance. Stimulates natural crystals in body tissue and fluids to resonate at new healing frequency. The greatest of all healing stones. Acts as an amplifier for psychic energy and aids meditation and visualization.

CARNELIAN: Improves physical energy, confidence, assertiveness; stimulate appetite, emotions, sexuality.

FLUORITE: Assists the conscious mind and body in analyzing conditions and situations in a rational and non-emotional manner, it enables detachment of the mind from the emotions so that the thought process can utilize the intuitive in achieving a higher level of self understanding. Mental clarity. Helps to tap creative resources and experience the inner self. Enhances spiritual energy work, focuses the will and balances the psyche. Enhances ability to concentrate.

GOLDSTONE: Uplifting, reduces tension and stomach problems.

HEMATITE: One of the most grounding of all stones. Condenses confusion into mental clarity, concentration, memory, practicality, helps study, bookkeeping, detail work, sound sleep. Confidence, will power, boldness. Egyptians used it to calm hysteria and anxiety. Helps adjust to being physical. Enables the psychic practitioner to unfocus from the physical world so as to receive psychic information. Aids in developing the psychic mental mind, optimism, grounds ideas, anti-depression. Calms and soothes, eases stress. Great stone for grounding.

JADE: Emotional balance, humility, harmony, wealth, longevity, compassion.

JASPER: (Yellow, orange, brown, green) Jasper is known as the "supreme nurturer" It reminds us that we are not here on this physical plane just for ourselves but also here to bring joy and substance to others, assisting others in releasing the bonds of negative energy. It is the stone that protects against negativity and helps one to be grounded to the stabilizing energy of the earth. Use this stone for long periods of hospitalization and when your energy feels low.

JASPER: (red) Powerful stone used for divination practice, worn to protect the individual during out of body experiences and vision quests by providing a solid grounding. It helps with conflict and aggression. Promotes grace and perseverance.

LAPIS LAZULI: Reduces anxiety, restlessness, insomnia, and shyness.

MALACHITE: Reduces depression & anger. Stimulates vision & concentration.

MOONSTONE: Soothes stress, anxiety, Enhances intuitive sensitivity via feelings and less overwhelmed by personal feelings. Greater flexibility and flow of life. For emotional balance, gracefulness. Balance of Ying-Yang energy. Can open your heart to love. It is also helpful in psychic work. It opens the spirit to the feminine aspect.

MOSS AGATE: Promotes agreeability, persuasiveness and strength in all endeavors. Improves self-esteem. Moss agate was used by the Native Americans as a power stone for the art of "cloud-busting" to bring rain. It is also said to help one in the acquisition of riches.

MOTHER OF PEARL: Wealth

ONYX: Protection. This stone helps to change bad habits, it is also an excellent grounding stone. Absorbs and flattens emotional intensity. Used for self-protection and to keep away bothersome relationships. Helps to release old relationships and keep away general negativity.

RHODONITE: Promotes self-esteem, self-worth and self-confidence, self-affirmation and self-love. Fosters ability to remain calm in arguments and resolve disagreements in a loving way.

ROSE QUARTZ: Emotional balance, love, beauty, peacefulness, kindness & self-esteem.

SAPPHIRE QUARTZ: A good healing stone to expand self expression and creativity, plus refining communication skills to new levels.

SNOWFLAKE OBSIDIAN: For grounding the physical and for protection. Used as a scrying tool to help the psychic unfocus from the physical and venture inward to receive information. Legendary dispeller of negativity, protects against nightmares and emotional draining.

SOLADITE: Healing of emotions and physical body. Assures clear communication. Eliminates guilt and fears and brings about clear vision. Elicits deep thought and calms overreaction by enabling one to think clearly.

TIGERSEYE: For protection, divination and inquiry into past or future lives. Clarity, optimism, and creativity. Enhances psychic ability. Stimulates wealth and helps to maintain it.

TOPAZ: The most powerful, electromagnetic of yellow/solar plexus gems. A strong, steady, high level gem for mental clarity, focus, perceptively, high level concepts, confidence, personal power, stamina. Helps with mood swings, insomnia, worries, fears, depression, exhaustion, nervous system stress, stomach anxiety. Radiates warmth, sun/light energy, protection. Brings emotions and thinking into balance. One can focus their desires through this stone, visual images in the mind are transformed into universal messages. Enables communication from other realms in the universe. Promotes peace and calms emotions, as well as promoting forgiveness.

TURQUOISE: A master healing stone that promotes spontaneity in romance and stimulates the initiation of romantic love. It balances and aligns all charkas and subtle

bodies and can bring all energies to a higher level. A highly
spiritual stone, yet grounding, it brings soothing energy
and peace of mind. It brings strength, wisdom, protection,
and positive thinking. A good general healer for all
illnesses and excellent conductor. This gentle, cool,
soothing stone is a Native American classic. For open
communication, creativity, serenity, spiritual bonding, and
upliftment. It opens the heart for giving/receiving. It
symbolizes our source (spirit/sky) and spiritual love for
healing, and help. Turquoise is the ancient absorber of
"negativity".

UNIKITE: Healing of the soul. Guide to transformation
and higher self. Reconciliation. Promotes balance and
emotional stability. Transforms negative emotions into
positive ones. A grounding stone.

CRYSTALS FOR SPECIFIC RESULTS

READINESS FOR ACTION: Amethyst, Ametrine, Fire Opal, Chrysoprase, Rhodonite, Turquoise

NEW BEGINNINGS: Garnet

CHEERFULNESS: Amber, Fire Opal

CREATIVITY: Ametrine, Amber, Garnet, Labradorite, Tourmaline

UNFINISHED BUSINESS: Aquamarine, Carnelian

FULFILLMENT OF DESIRES: Amber, Malachite, Hematite, Fire Opal

DEVOTION: Kunzite, Tourmaline

SOLVING DIFFICULTIES: Carnelian, Garnet, Moss Agate, Smokey Quartz, Tiger Eye

CONNECTION WITH EARTH: Petrified Wood

ENTHUSIASM: Aventurine, Fire Opal, Garnet, Labradorite, Rhodochrosite

FERTILITY: Chrysoprase, Imperial Toopaz, Moonstone, Rhodonite, Rose Quartz

FORESIGHT: Aquamarine, Turquoise

FRIENDSHIP: Emerald, Lapis Lazuli, Malachite, Peridot, Rhodonite, Watermelon Tourmaline

GOAL SETTING: Labradorite, Lepidolite, Watermelon Tourmaline

INDUSTRIOUSNESS: Rhodochrosite

INTUITION: Amethyst, Amazonite, Ametrine, Petrified Wood, Kunzite, Labradorite, Moonstone, Turquoise

LOVE: Chrysoprase, Emerald, Moonstone, Rhodochrosite, Rose Quartz, Ruby, Watermelon Tourmaline

LUCK: Agate, Ametrine, Aventurine, Amber, Chrysoprase, Garnet, Malachite, Moonstone, Sunstone, Turquoise

INCREASE MOTIVATION: Amber, Chrysoprase

ORDER: Aquamarine, Fluorite, Sodalite

POSITIVE ATTITUDE TOWARDS LIFE: Malachite, Chrysoprase, Imperial Topaz, Rhodochrosite, Sunstone

PROTECTION: Agate, Lepidolite, Smokey Quartz, Serpentine, Tiger Eye, Turquoise, Black Tourmaline, Watermelon Tourmaline

SELF-CONFIDENCE: Calcite, Citrine, Fluorite, Garnet, Imperial Topaz, Sunstone

STAMINS: Aquamarine, Garnet, Red Jasper

LOGICAL THINKING: Agate, Chrysoprase, Citrine, Kunzite, Lepidolite, Black Tourmaline

SPIRTUAL PATHWAYS & PRIESTHOOD

WHY DO PEOPLE CHOOSE THIS PATH?

There is no one answer to this question. Some choose
Wicca because they are frustrated with the patriarchal
nature of the three major Abrahamic religions. To some, it
is a calling: there are those who knew that Wicca was the
correct path for them the minute they heard the Wiccan
Rede or learned the 13 goals of Wiccans. Some do not feel
connected to the so-called major religions, and their thirst
for spirituality leads them to Wicca. Still others have
always praised the Earth, sensed Goddess energy, and felt a
special connection to nature, and later learned that there
was a religion that could develop and fine tune their
feelings and skills.

No one can tell you, or anyone else, what the correct
religion is. If Wicca feels right, you'll know.

RIGORS OF PASTORAL DUTIES

The duties of the Priestess or the Priest vary greatly according to the individual coven, and the type of Wicca to which a coven adheres. In a Dianic Wiccan coven, for instance, there will be no Priest, and the duty of spiritual leadership will not be shared.

In general, the Priest or the Priestess is the most studied and most experienced of the coven members. It is his or her duty to lead rituals and ceremonies, to offer spiritual and personal guidance to members of the coven, and to act as a model and example to others.

The Priest or Priestess may serve as the vessel to the Goddess or God in the Drawing Down of the Sun and the Moon. He or she may also be responsible for selecting appropriate places of worship, and for assessing the spiritual willingness of new coven members.

The Priestess and Priest are charged with ruling and governing the Circle with justice and with love, resolving conflicts amongst coven members, acting as a representative for the coven if necessary.

Clergy members in Wicca do not have the authority to "excommunicate" members, nor forbid them from practicing. They may not deviate from the Wiccan Rede or Creed when dealing with conflict resolution, or disciplining coven members. In short, the Priest and the Priestess do their best to walk in the path illuminated by the God and the Goddess, and to bring their covens together for worship, rituals, and general merrymaking.

SOME SIGNS & SYMBOLS

	The God, The Horned God, the horned moon, masculine
	The Goddess, The Triple Goddess, Represents 3 aspects of the moon and womankind, feminine
	Cauldron
	Pentacle
	Pentagram

	Air
	Fire
	Earth
	Water
	Moon
	Sun

	The wheel of the year, marks the Holy Days in the Wicca Ritual Calendar
	Mercury
	Venus
	Earth
	Mars

♃	Jupiter
♄	Saturn
♅	Uranus
♆	Neptune
♇	Pluto

	Spirit or Hexagram
	Spirit Circle

MORE RECEIPES

Crafts and cooking are one of the most fun parts of celebrating Wiccan holidays! Those who are not confident in their culinary skills, do not despair. It is not mandatory to whip up a feast in honor of any holiday; but many covens regard food as a central part of holiday celebrations. No one will think less of you if you choose to bring dried apples to a celebration instead of, say, apple pie. If you would like ideas as to what sorts of foods might be appropriate to prepare, however, here are a couple of ideas that are simple, yet impressive, to prepare, as well as my favorite folk remedies.

SUMMER BREAD PUDDING

6 slices of thick, good quality day-old brioche bread

8 large eggs

¼ cup white sugar

2 tbsp brown sugar

4 cups milk

1 ½ tsp vanilla extract

4 peaches

2 c. sliced strawberries

Nutmeg

Cinnamon

Arrange the brioche slices on a baking sheet, and lightly toast for five minutes to dry them out and increase their ability to absorb. Remove; set aside.

Crack eggs into a mixing bowl and whisk with the sugar, milk, vanilla, and salt.

Place the toasted bread slices into a baking dish, trimming them if they extend over the top of the pan. Pour the egg mixture over the bread. Let it sit for at least an hour, but ideally, over night. Cover the dish with aluminum foil, and bake in a preheated oven at 350 degrees.

The time it will take to bake depends on whether or not it was refrigerated overnight. Start with one hour. After one hour, check to see if its done. If it is done, poke around the bread with a fork or a knife to see if the egg mixture is still liquid. If it does, it needs more baking.

Remove from the oven. Sprinkle very lightly with nutmeg and cinnamon, and then layer with the peaches and strawberries. It's now ready to serve!

THE POOR WITCH'S CHEESECAKE

1 c. blueberries, strawberries, peaches, or banana

1 block cream cheese, softened

1 package graham crackers, crumbled

3 tbsp honey

This is a simple, quick dessert that can be made with fruit from almost any season.

Simply mix the fruit with the cream cheese and crumbled graham crackers. Scoop into goblets, add a drizzle of honey and a wedge of graham cracker as decoration, and serve!

WINTER HOT TODDY

Brandy
Cloves
Cinnamon
Lemon juice

I was suffering from a horrific cold when I was in Ireland. A barkeep whipped this up for me and I was right as rain in about an hour!

Heat the brandy (or whisky, if you wish) in a saucepan. Add a pinch of cloves, and let it sit on the stove top for a few minutes so the cloves can flavor the liquor. Add a teaspoon of lemon juice. Drink, take a hot bath (taking care to get someone to supervise you if you fear you are too drowsy to do so safely) and rest. You will feel much, much better very soon.

SHOOTERS FOR THE SICK WITCH

Cayenne pepper

Tapatio sauce

Garlic clove

Hot water

Lemon wedge

Chop a garlic clove into tiny slivers, using a garlic press if possible. Put in the bottom of a shot glass or bucket glass. Add a few drops of tapatio. Pour hot water onto it, add a pinch of cayenne pepper. and squeeze lemon juice in it. Now drink it in one shot! Your sinuses should be cleared immediately. Don't do this if you have a flu though. Just a sinus infection or a cold. Wassabi also works well.

ANT KILLER

Cinnamon

I hate ants. But I hate Raid even more. If your house becomes infested with ants, sprinkle cinnamon on their point of origin. It will stun them, and they won't come back. Plus your kitchen will smell nice!

REFERENCES

Cunningham's "Encyclopedia of Magical Herbs" ©1994, Llewellyn Publications

Silver Ravenwolf's "To Ride a Silver Broomstick" © 1993 Llewellyn Publications

Mrs. M. Grieve's "A Modern Herbal" ©1931, Harcourt Brace

"A Handbook of Native American Herbs" © 1992 Shambhala Publications,

Back to Eden © 1981 Mass Market Publications,

My own experiences

INDEX